Venice

Italy

EVERYMAN
CITY GUIDES

ISBN 1 84159 028 2

First published April 2001

Originally published in France by
Nouveaux Loisirs, a subsidiary of
Gallimard, Paris 2000, and in Italy
by Touring Editore, Srl.,
Milano 2000
Copyright © 2000
Nouveaux Loisirs,
Touring Editore. Srl.

SERIES EDITORS
Anne-Josyane Magniant/Marisa Bassi
VENICE EDITION:
TCI: Asterisco srl, Milan
GRAPHICS
Yann Le Duc with Isabelle
Dubois-Dumée
LAYOUT: Fiammetta Badalato
MINI-MAPS: Fiammetta Badalato and
Flavio Badalato
STREET MAPS:
Touring Club Italiano

Translated by Sara Harris and
Simon Knight in association with
First Edition Translations Ltd,
Cambridge, UK

Typeset by The Write Idea in
association with First Edition
Translations Ltd, Cambridge, UK

Printed in Italy by
Editoriale Lloyd

Authors
VENICE

Things you need to know/ Further afield:
Pietro Boratto (1)
Though a native of Padua province, it is in
Venice, where he was a student, that Pietro
Boratto feels really at home. He has
written a number of guides for the Italian
Touring Club (TCI), and thoroughly enjoys
the traveling involved.

Where to stay:
Teresa Cremona (2)
Teresa Cremona lives in Rome and has
been involved in tourism since the 1970s.
She managed the Rome office of
Mondadori Viaggi and the marketing
department of Wagons-Lits Tourisme. She
has worked with the TCI for several years,
selecting and inspecting hundreds of
establishments each year.

Where to eat:
Luigi Cremona (3)
An engineer and journalist with a special
interest in wine, Luigi Cremona has worked
with the TCI for many years, coordinating
guide book projects, writing articles for
trade magazines and organizing special
events.

After dark / Where to shop:
Valentina Casavola (4)
A philosophy graduate from Rome,
Valentina Casavola has edited a number of
works on tourism and gastronomy. For
some years she has been involved in movies
and the theater, organizing international
conferences and events and publishing
material in this field.

Where to shop:
Silvana Marzagalli (5)
Silvana Marzagalli has been a TCI
consultant for many years. Since taking a
language degree in Venice, she has
specialized in art history and literature. She
has been responsible for a number of
publications, including museum and
exhibition catalogs.

Symbols

- ☎ telephone
- → fax
- ● price or price range
- ◷ opening hours
- ▤ credit cards accepted
- ▤ credit cards not accepted
- ▼ toll-free number
- @ e-mail/website address
- ★ tips and recommendations

Access

- Ⓜ subway stations
- 🚍 bus (or tram)
- 🅿 private parking
- 🚶 parking attendant
- ⓚ no facilities for the disabled
- 🚆 train
- 🚗 car
- 🚢 boat

Hotels

- ☏ telephone in room
- ▥ fax in room on request
- ⬛ minibar
- ⬛ television in room
- ▥ air-conditioned rooms
- ⓘ 24-hour room service
- ⬛ caretaker
- ⬛ babysitting
- ⬛ meeting room(s)
- ⬛ no pets
- ⬛ breakfast
- ⬛ open for tea/coffee
- ⬛ restaurant
- ⬛ live music
- ⬛ disco
- ⬛ garden, patio or terrace
- ⬛ gym, fitness club
- ⬛ swimming pool, sauna

Restaurants

- ⬛ vegetarian food
- ⬛ view
- ⬛ formal dress required
- ⬛ smoking area
- ⬛ bar

Museums and galleries

- ⬛ on-site store(s)
- ⬛ guided tours
- ⬛ café

Stores

- ⬛ branches, outlets

The Insider's Guide is made up of **8 sections**, each indicated by a different color.

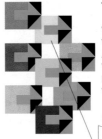

Things you need to know (mauve)
Where to stay (blue)
Where to eat (red)
After dark (pink)
What to see (green)
Further afield (orange)
Where to shop (yellow)
Finding your way (purple)

San Marco
piazza San M

Practical information is given for each particular establishment: opening times, prices, ways of paying, different services available

Where to sho

Bargain!
This star marks good value hotels and restaurants.

How to use this guide

In the area
- ▸ **Where to stay:** ➡ 20 ➡ 34
- ▸ **Where to eat:** ➡ 40 ➡ 54 ➡ 56
- ▸ **After dark:** ➡ 64 ➡ 68
- ▸ **What to see:** ➡ 78 ➡ 82 ➡ 110

The section **" In the area"** refers you (➡ 00) to other establishments that are covered in a different section of the guide but found in the same area of the city.

an Marco / Castello   **E** B-C 1-2-3

The small map shows all the establishments mentioned and others described elsewhere but found "in the area", by the color of the section.

The name of the district is given above the map. A grid reference (**A** B-C 2) enables you to find it in the section on Maps at the end of the book.

Not forgetting
- ■ **Sigfrido Cipolato** (5) calle C.

The section " Not forgetting" lists other useful addresses in the same area.

The opening page to each section contains an index ordered alphabetically (Getting there), by subject or by district (After dark) as well as useful addresses and advice.

The section "Things you need to know" covers information on getting to Venice and day-to-day life in the city.

Theme pages introduce a selection of establishments on a given topic.

The "Maps" section of this guide contains 5 street plans of Venice followed by a detailed index.

Access for the disabled

Despite the hundreds of bridges, it is not difficult for disabled people to get around in Venice. The ACTV ➡ 12 distributes a free brochure setting out obstacle-free itineraries. For further information, apply to the city hall ☎ 041 976435.

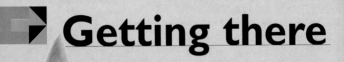

Getting there

Help for tourists in distress

When your attention is focused on the sights of so beautiful a city, you can easily forget to keep an eye on your purse or wallet... To help tourists in trouble, the APT (the city's tourist office) ➡ 15 has organized a freephone number. ⓥ 800 355920.

Expensive to feed the pigeons!

A municipal bylaw makes it an offense to feed pigeons within the city limits. Offenders may have to pay a hefty fine (up to 1,000,000 lire)! Only Piazza San Marco, the Piazzetta, the royal gardens and the Riva degli Schiavoni – between the Ponte della Paglia and the Ponte del Vino – are exempted from this ban.

Advantages for young people

If you are under 29, you qualify for reductions in Venice's museums, hotels and restaurants. Just ask for a **Carta Giovani** at the city hall, at the **Punta Informagiovani** office *Corte Contarina, San Marco 1529* ☎ *041 2747637* 🕒 *Mon. and Fri. 10am–1pm; Tue. 3–6pm; Thu. 10am–1pm, 3–6pm.*

47 Things
you need to know

Porter!

If you have heavy luggage, call the **Cooperativa Trasbagagli** ☎ *041 713719* 🕒 *7.30am–8pm*. The charge depends on your destination and the weight of your luggage: for example, from the Santa Lucia railroad station to Piazza San Marco costs roughly 50,000 lire. A supplement is payable before 7am and after 8pm.

"Acqua alta"

In November and December, Venice suffers from flooding whenever there are high tides – *acque alte*. Kit yourself out with rubber boots and, when the alarm is sounded, follow the itineraries shown on the map ➡ 15; For further information: **Centro previsioni e segnalazioni maree** ☎ *041 2748787* 🕒 *8am–2pm* ☎ *041 5206344* (recorded message).

Basic facts

Marco Polo International Airport, the third most important Italian airport in terms of passengers, is situated at Tessera, 7½ miles north of Venice. Recently enlarged, it handles air traffic from all over the northeast of the peninsula, with direct flights to major international airports. A link road

Getting there

Getting there

Information
☎ 041 2609260
@ www.veniceairport.it
🕐 8am–8pm; Sat. 8am–4pm
Closed Sun.

Arrivals
☎ 041 2609240

Lost property
☎ 041 2606436

Left luggage
🕐 6am–9pm
● 3,500 lire per item per day

Post office
☎ 041 5415900
🕐 8.10am–1.30pm; Sat., last day of month 8.10am–noon; closed Sun.

Banks
🕐 8.30am–1.30pm, 2.45–3.45pm; closed Sat., Sun.; 24-hr ATM, bureau de change

Venezia Turismo
☎ 041 5415911

Banca di Roma
☎ 041 5415498

Banca Antoniana Popolare Veneta
☎ 041 5415904

Change
Venezia Turismo
☎ 041 5415471
🕐 9am–10.30pm; Sun. 9.30am–10.30pm

Emergencies
☎ 041 2606335

Car rental (1)
Avis
☎ 041 5415030
🕐 8am–midnight

Hertz
☎ 041 5416075
🕐 8am–midnight

Maggiore
☎ 041 5415040
🕐 8am–11.30pm

Europcar
☎ 041 5415654
🕐 8am–midnight

Sixt
☎ 041 5415570
🕐 8am–11.45pm, Sat., Sun. 8.30am–10pm

Tourist information
APT/IAT office
☎ 041 5298711
🕐 9am–8pm

Hotel reservations (2)
Hotel association
☎ 041 5415017
🕐 9am–10pm

Sheraton – Ciga Hotels
☎ 041 5415041
🕐 8am–7pm

Departures

Information
☎ 041 2606111
🕐 8am–8pm; Sat. 8am–4pm; closed Sun.

Flights
☎ 041 2609260

Departures
☎ 041 2609250

Ticket sales (3)
☎ 041 2606428
🕐 Mon.–Thu. and Sun. 5.30am–9.45pm; Fri.–Sat. 5.30am–9pm

Hotel
Fly Hotel
via Triestina 170 Tessera
☎ 041 5415022
➠ 041 5415286

Getting to and from the center

From the airport
Bus
ACTV
Urban bus line 5 to and from Piazzale Roma; journey time 20 mins; departures approx. every 30 mins from the

leading to the northern-Italian highway network opened in 1999.

airport, every 50 mins to the airport. ☼ daily 4.05am–1.10am from the airport, 4.40am–12.40am from the city
Tickets (4)
Box ACTV
☎ 041 5415180
☼ 8am–midnight; / ☎ 041 5287886
☼ 7.30am–8pm
● 1,500 lire
ATVO
Bus to and from Piazzale Roma; journey time 20 mins; departures approx. every 30 mins from the airport, every 50 mins to the airport.
☼ 8.30am–12.20am from the airport, 5.30am–8.40pm from the city
Tickets (5)

ATVO office
☎ 041 5415180
☼ 8am–midnight / ☎ 041 5205530
☼ 6.40am–7.40pm
● 5,000 lire (tickets can also be bought on the bus)
Motorboat
Airport to Piazza San Marco: terminates at Zattere, stopping at Murano, Lido, Arsenale; to airport: departs from Zattere, stopping at Piazza San Marco, Arsenale, Lido and Murano. Journey time: 1 hr 25mins approx.; departures every 50 mins approx.
☼ 6.15–12.05am from the airport, 4.35am–10.35pm

Tickets (7)
Alilaguna office
☎ 041 5415180
☼ 8am–midnight / ☎ 041 5235775
☼ 8am–11pm
● 17,000 lire
Taxis (6)
Just outside arrivals at airport; from Piazzale Roma; 24-hr service.
Radiotaxi
☎ 041 936222
● 50,000 lire approx.
Water-taxi
Consorzio Motoscafi Venezia
☎ 041 5222303
☼ 24-hr service
● 140,000 lire approx.

Airlines

Italy
Alitalia
☎ 147 865641 (Bookings)

British Airways
☎ 167 287287 (Bookings) 041 5415629 (Offices)
Delta
☎ 800 864114 (Bookings)
Go
☎ 147 887766 (Bookings)
KLM
☎ 02 216969 (Bookings) 041 5416111 (Offices)
UK
Alitalia
☎ 020 8745 8200
➡ 020 7602 5584 / 020 7646 0471
British Airways
☎ 0345 222111
Lufthansa
☎ 0345 737747
US
Alitalia
☎ 800 223 5730
British Airways
☎ 800 AIRWAYS
Delta
☎ 800 221 1212

Getting there

By train

All trains arriving at, and departing from Santa Lucia train station also stop at Mestre.

Santa Lucia train station (1)

Information
☎ 041 5245346
🕐 7.15am–9.15pm
FS Informa
🆅 147888088
🕐 7am–9pm
International green number: information for entire Italian railroad network.

Ticket sales
☎ 041 716601
🕐 5.50am–9.30pm

Reservations
🕐 7am–8.30pm

Waiting room
🕐 5am–12.30am

Left luggage
🕐 3.45am–1.20am
● 5,000 lire per item per part/ whole of 12-hr period

Lost property
☎ 041 785238
🕐 8am–4pm; closed Sat., Sun.

Banks
Istituto Bancario S. Paolo di Torino
☎ 041 716854
🕐 8.25am–1.25pm, 2.40–4.10pm; closed Sat., Sun.

Bureau de Change

☎ 041 5674546
🕐 5.50am–9.30pm

Tourist and hotel information
☎ 041 719078
🕐 8.10am–6.50pm

Railroad police
☎ 041 785620

By car

Mestre is the gateway to the Lagoon for car drivers. Watch out for very heavy traffic at interchanges and

on the National Road 11 to Padua!

Expressways (2)

A4
'Serenissima': westward to Milan, eastward to Trieste.

A13
Near Padua a link road connects the A4 with the A13 to Bologna.

A27
Shortly after the Mestre Est (East) exit from the A4, exit for expressway to

port, on the Giudecca Canal.

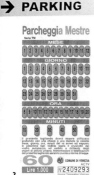

Vittorio Veneto, Belluno and, eventually, the Dolomites.

Parking (3)
If space is available, vehicles can be left in car parks in Piazzale Roma or Tronchetto. Parking in Mestre is recommended; take the train or ACTV bus onward.

Mestre
Park and Pay in blue zones; to pay, purchase (and display) 'Gratta e parcheggi' (Scratch & Park) tickets on sale at tobacconists and authorized kiosks.

Underground parking
piazzale Candiani
☎ 041 976844
🕐 6.45am–12.30am
● 16,000 lire per day

High-rise parking with parking meters
piazzale Santa Maria dei Battuti, piazzale Altinate, piazzale Einaudi
🕐 24 hrs
● 1,000 lire per hr

Tronchetto
Long-stay car parks

☎ 041 5207555
🕐 24 hrs
● 30,000 lire per day

Piazzale Roma (4)
Municipal car park
☎ 041 2727301
🕐 24 hrs
● 30,000 lire per day

Sant'Andrea car park
piazzale Roma
☎ 041 2727304
🕐 24 hrs
● 8,000 lire per 2 hrs

By boat
Cruise liners moor in the port; ferries leave for Croatia, Greece and Turkey.

Port (5)
Stazione Marittima (Harbor train station)
Zattere Dorsoduro 1401 30123 Venezia
☎ 041 5334111
➡ 041 5334254

Harbor-master
☎ 041 5205600

Frontier police
☎ 041 2723211

In Venice people get around mainly on foot, and this is what distinguishes the native-born Venetian from the tourist: he can get across town in less than a half-hour... without getting lost. As a tourist, you would do well to follow the yellow street signs marking the main thoroughfares.

Getting around

ACTV

Vaporetti and motoscafi (1) (water buses)

Public transport throughout the Venice area is run by the Azienda Corsorzio Trasporti Veneziano (ACTV). The city center is served by relatively slow *vaporetti*, and by *motoscafi*, which make fewer stops. A new kind of boat, the 'Liuto' or Low Urban Transport Water Omnibus, which respects the fragile environment of the lagoon, is now in service.

Motonavi (2) (longer-distance ferry boats)

Serve the Lido and the islands of the lagoon.

Information
Piazzale Roma
☎ 041 5287886
@ www.actv.it
⏱ 7.30am–8pm

Times of operation
⏱ 4am–midnight approx.

Line 1
The 'accelerated' service is not very appropriately named: it stops at every landing stage between Piazzale Roma and the Lido. However, it is the best – and cheapest – way to see the palaces along the Grand Canal.

Line N
A night-time service calling at the main stops.
⏱ midnight–4am approx.

Seasonal lines
Between April and October a double service operates on the most used routes to cope with the tourist influx.

Tickets (3)
Buy your ticket at the ticket office of the landing stage where you intend to board the boat.
● 6,000 lire one way; 10,000 lire round trip

Booklet of tickets
● 50,000 lire for 10 journeys

Group tickets
● 15,000 lire for 3 people; 20,000 lire for 4 people; 25,000 lire for 5 people

Season tickets
● 18,000 lire for 24 hours; 35,000 lire for 72 hours; 60,000 lire for one week

Crossing the Grand Canal
There are three bridges: Scalzi, Rialto and Accademia. To avoid a lot of walking, you can

You can also take a *vaporetto* for traveling up and down the Grand Canal or, if you can afford it, a more romantic gondola!

hop back and forth by taking line 1.

● *3,000 lire one way; 5,000 lire round trip.*

Reductions
Holders of a Carta Giovani ➡ 7 and groups (of at least 20 people) all qualify for reductions.

Lost property
☎ 041 2722179

Taxis

A good way of getting around, but considerably more expensive than public transport. Before going aboard, check that your taxi is 'official' and that it has a meter.

Landing stages (4)
Piazzale Roma

☎ 041 716922
Railroad station
☎ 041 716124
Rialto
☎ 041 5230575
San Marco
☎ 041 5229750
Lido
☎ 041 5260049
Radio taxis
☎ 041 5222303
🕐 *24-hr service*
Consorzio Motoscafi Venezia
☎ 041 5222303
● *27,000 lire for the first 7 mins + 450 lire for every 15 seconds thereafter (municipal rate); from Piazzale Roma to the railroad station to Piazza San Marco you are likely to pay around 90,000 lire for 4 people (luggage extra).*

Gondolas (5)

A delightful way to see Venice, but make sure you negotiate the price before climbing aboard!

Ente della Gondola
☎ 041 5285075
Reservations
Bacino Orseolo
☎ 041 5289316
Calle Vallaresso
☎ 041 5205275
● *70,000 lire for 45 mins and 40,000 lire for each additional 30-mins period; 80,000 lire at night; 5 people maximum.*

Gondola ferries (6)
This is a way of crossing the Grand Canal at a

reasonable price. To find the appropriate ('Stazi') landing stages, follow the yellow 'traghetto' signs.

'Stazi'
(see map)
San Marcuola-Fondaco dei Turchi (7)
🕐 *7.45am–1.20pm*
Santa Sofia-Pescaria (8)
🕐 *7.45am–8pm*
Riva del Carbon-Riva del Vin (9)
🕐 *7.45am–1.20pm*
San Tomà-Sant'Angelo (10)
🕐 *7.45am–8pm*
San Barnaba-San Samuele (11)
🕐 *7.45am–1.20pm*
Santa Maria del Giglio-La Salute (12)
🕐 *7.45am–1.20pm*

Basic facts

Venice has fewer than 70,000 inhabitants, but is visited by several million tourists each year. A living museum, it is also a thriving community and has developed the infrastructure to meet the needs of its people and its many visitors.

Getting by

Money

Currency (1)

The currency unit is the Italian lira (LIT). Notes come in 1,000, 2,000, 5,000, 10,000, 50,000, 100,000 and 500,000-lire denominations. There are also 50, 100, 200, 500 and 1,000-lire coins.

Banks

The main Italian banks have branches in Venice. Their exchange rates are often more favorable than those offered by bureaux de change.

🕐 8.30am–1.30pm, 2.45–3.45pm *(afternoon opening times vary from bank to bank); closed Sat., Sun.*

Bureaux de change (2)

Bureaux de change can be found near the main tourist attractions, as well as at the airport and railroad station. Money can be obtained from cash dispensers 24 hours a day.

Credit cards (3)

Widely accepted by shops, hotels and restaurants. To report the loss of a card:
Visa-Mastercard
☎ 167 821001
American Express
☎ 167 821001

The media

Regional daily newspapers (4)

Il Gazzettino

is the most widely read daily.

International newspapers and magazines

A wide choice can be found on the news-stands around Piazza San Marco and the Accademia.

Station news-stand
☎ 041 716209
🕐 6am–9pm

Radio

In addition to the public-service frequencies of the RAI and Radio Capodistria, there are many private radio stations.

Television

There are three national channels (RAI Uno, Due and Tre), three private Mediaset channels and two

TMC channels, as well as local ones.

Internet

Surf the web in Internet cafés, and at the Querini Stampalia Foundation
➡ 110.
Web sites
Venice city hall
@ www.comune.venezia.it

Telephones

All Venice numbers now begin with 041.

Calling from Venice

To call abroad, dial 00 followed by the national code (e.g. UK 44, US and Canada 1), then the subscriber's number.

Calling Venice from abroad

Dial 00–39 from the UK or 011–39

from the US and Canada, then the subscriber's 10-digit number.

General information
☎ 176

Collect calls
☎ 170

Public telephones (5)
Coin-operated, or buy a phone card from news-stands or tobacconists' (5,000, 10,000 or 15,000 lire). Some telephones accept credit cards.

Postal Services

Central post office (6)
Fondaco dei Tedeschi

Near the Rialto
San Marco 5554
☎ 041 271711
🕐 8.10am–6pm; last day of the month 8.10am–noon; closed Sun.

Tourist offices

APT/IAT
Castello 4421
☎ 041 5298711
➡ 041 5230399
@ apt-06@mail.
regione.veneto.it,
www.provincia.
venezia.it/aptve
Piazza San Marco
San Marco 71/F
☎ 041 5298711
🕐 9.30am–3.30pm
Palazzina del Santi
☎ 041 5298711
🕐 10am–6pm
Santa Lucia railroad station

☎ 041 5298711
🕐 8am–7pm
Venice Lido
Viale Santa Maria Elisabetta 6/A
☎ 041 5298711
🕐 tourist season
Mestre
Rotonda Marghera Villabona
☎ 041 5298711
🕐 tourist season

Emergency services

Police
Prefecture
☎ 041 271511
Military police
☎ 112
Fire brigade (7)
☎ 115
Police emergency
☎ 113
Municipal police (8)
☎ 041 2748203
Foreigners' help-line
☎ 041 5204777

Health services

Emergencies
☎ 041 5294517
Municipal hospital
Campo Santissimi Giovanni e Paolo Cannaregio
☎ 041 5294111
Ambulances
☎ 041 5230000
Duty doctors (public holidays and night-time)
Only in emergencies
☎ 041 5294060
🕐 8pm–8am
Public toilets
In the more central parts of town, they are equipped for the disabled.
🕐 Apr. 15– Oct. 15:
8am–8pm;
Apr. 14–Nov. 16:
8am–7pm
● 500 lire

Where to stay

A sense of history
Immortalized by artists and writers
as diverse as Canaletto and Thomas
Mann, the 'bride of the sea' has
attracted dreamers from around
the world for generations. Ever
since she first dominated the
Adriatic, and the silk roads opened
up by Marco Polo, Venice has
remained a city of luxury and
romance, revealed by the rich
architecture of her buildings and
bridges and the interiors still
adorned with riches of the East...

An aristocratic old lady

Venice is an old lady desperately short of space. Her ancient palaces are not always equipped with the latest domestic technology. So do not be too disappointed by the smallness of hotel rooms or the lack of modern facilities in some historic residences. This is the price you pay for the privilege of staying in such a unique city.

47

Hotels

Hotel rates

The prices quoted are for a double room with breakfast (continental or buffet). Not surprisingly, accommodation in Venice is expensive, particularly at Christmas, in February (carnival time) and in summer, when the city is full of tourists. It is worth enquiring about out-of-season possibilities, when some hoteliers offer attractive rates.

Camp site and youth hostel

In summer, camping can be a very pleasant option:
Marina di Venezia *via Montello 6, 30010 Punta Sabbioni, Cavallino/Treporti* ☎ *041 5300955* ➡ *041 966036* ;
If you are on a restricted budget, the **Youth hostel** is open all the year round *fondamenta della Croce, Giudecca, Dorsoduro 86* ☎ *041 5238211* ➡ *041 5235689*

Whether large or small, luxury palaces or family *pensioni*, many of Venice's hotels have an aristocratic charm: painted wooden furniture decorated with floral motifs, valuable wall hangings, coffered ceilings, sparkling Murano-glass chandeliers... Enjoy a romantic interlude in an atmosphere worthy of *The Thousand and One Nights*.

➡ Where to stay

Danieli (1)
riva degli Schiavoni, Castello 4196, 30122
☎ 041 5226480 ➡ 041 5200208

🚉 San Zaccaria **231 rooms** ●●●●● *11 suites* 1,100,000 lire 🛏 72,000 lire ▣ ① ▣ ☎ 🏧 📶 📺 safe 🍽 La Terrazza ⏱ noon–3pm, 7–10.30pm ⏳ 🍸 Dandolo ⏱ 9.30–1am 🎵 ⏳ 🖼 ✂ ♿ ✖ ✚ banqueting suite 💱 ✖ ⛷ @ res072_danieli@sheraton.com

Founded in 1822, the Danieli is undoubtedly one of the most famous hotels in the world. The Gothic building it occupies has a tall, pink façade, decorated with contrasting white stone lacework, and looks out over St Mark's basin. ★ Among its many attractions are the sumptuously furnished public rooms and bedrooms, typifying the splendor of the City of the Doges. The gourmet restaurant has a stunning view over the lagoon.

Gritti Palace (2)
campo Santa Maria del Giglio, San Marco 2467, 30124
☎ 041 794611 ➡ 041 5200942

🚉 Santa Maria del Giglio, San Marco **93 rooms** ●●●●● *6 suites* 2,420,000 lire 🛏 46,200 lire ▣ ① ▣ ☎ 🏧 📶 📺 safe 🍽 Club del Doge ⏱ 12.30–2.30pm, 7–10.30pm ⏳ 🍸 Longhi ⏱ 11–12.30am 🎵 ⏳ ▣ 11–12.30am ⏳ 🖼 ✂ ♿ ✖ ✚ banqueting suite ✖ ⛷ @ Res073_GrittiPalace@sheraton.com

Some 50 years ago the palace of Doge Andrea Gritti (14th century) was turned into a luxury hotel. Every care was taken to retain the atmosphere of an aristocratic residence, and valuable tapestries, soft carpets, stuccos and frescos adorn the public areas and the restaurant. ★ The magnificent rooms are furnished with antiques, while the water-level terrace, where Hemingway used to enjoy being idle, is magical at sunset.

The majestic staircase in the Danieli's entrance hall is a prelude to the opulence of the bedrooms and suites.

Hotel Cipriani (3)
fondamenta delle Zitelle, Giudecca, Dorsoduro 10, 30133
☎ 041 5207744 ➞ 041 5203930

Zitelle **58 rooms** ●●●● 48 suites 2,500,000 lire ⚑ ▣ closed Nov.–Mar. 🕐 7am–midnight 📷 ▥ ▤ ▥ safe ☷ Cipriani 🕐 8–10.30pm ⚡ ☷ Cip's 🕐 12.30–3pm, 7.30–10pm ⚡ ♫ 🍸 Gabbiano 🕐 10pm–1.30am ⚡ ▣ 🕐 10.30am–6pm ⚡ 🍸 San Giorgio 🕐 6–10pm ⚡ ♨ ✕ ♿ ✕ banqueting suite ♨ ⚑ 1–3pm ✕ ▦ ✖ ✕ ✖ @ info@hotelcipriani.it ⚑ Palazzo Vendramin, 3 rooms and 7 suites ⚑ Il Palazzetto, 5 suites

A superb location on the southeast shore of Giudecca; Piazza San Marco only 5 minutes away by private motor boat shuttle service; a heated sea water swimming pool, the only one of its kind in Venice, and a first class restaurant: these are just some of the advantages of this dream hotel where members of the international jet set stay. Such success has meant that a modern 'annex', the Palazzo Vendramin had to be opened. ★ There is a little harbor where boats can moor for up to 20 minutes.

Grand Hotel Palazzo dei Dogi (4)
fondamenta Madonna dell'Orto, Cannaregio 3500, 30121
☎ 041 2208111 ➞ 041 722278

Madonna dell'Orto, San Marcuola **75 rooms** ●●●● 11 suites 900,000 lire ⚑ ▣ 🕐 ▣ 📷 ▥ ▤ ▥ safe ☷ La Zoia 🕐 7–10.30am, noon–2.30pm, 7–10pm ⚡ ▣ ♫ 🍸 Tintoretto 🕐 10am–midnight ⚡ ▣ ♫ ♨ ✕ ✕ ✚ banqueting suite ▦ ✖ ✕ @ grand.hoteldeidogi@boscolo.com

This hotel opened in July 1998. It was once an embassy and, later, a convent. The bedrooms, in Venetian style, with Murano glass chandeliers and Baroque stucco, offer a very romantic view of Murano and the northern lagoon. ★ An authentic Venetian setting, little known to tourists.

Where to stay

Bauer Grünwald (5)
campo San Moisè, San Marco 1459, 30124
☎ 041 5207022 ➡ 041 5207557

🔲 *San Marco 136 rooms* ●●●●● *60 suites 650,000 lire* 🔲 *60,000 lire* 🔲 🔲 🔲 🔲 🔲 *Bauer* 🔲 *noon–3pm, 7–10pm* 🔲 🔲 *De Pisis* 🔲 *noon–3pm, 7.30–10pm* 🔲 *La Terrazza* 🔲 *10am–1am* 🔲 🔲 🔲 🔲 *on request* 🔲 *banqueting suite* 🔲 🔲 🔲 🔲 @ *booking@bauervenezia.it*

None of the fin-de-siècle atmosphere was lost during the Bauer's 1999 restoration, when a VIP wing was added. Opt for a room with balcony for the view over St Mark's basin and the serenades of the gondoliers.

Hotel San Zulian (6)
calle degli Specchieri, San Marco 534/535, 30124
☎ 041 5225872 ➡ 041 5232265

🔲 *San Marco, Rialto 20 rooms* ●● 🔲 🔲 🔲 *7am–midnight* 🔲 🔲 🔲 🔲 *safe* 🔲 🔲 🔲 @ *h.sanzulian@iol.it, www.venere.it/venezia/san_zulian*

The hotel offers the atmosphere and the hospitality of a private residence. Pleasant rooms in pastel colors and with period furniture. A very affordable place to stay, next to no distance from Piazza San Marco.

Monaco & Grand Canal (7)
calle Vallaresso, San Marco 1325, 30124
☎ 041 5200211 ➡ 041 5200501

🔲 *San Marco 64 rooms* ●●●●● *7 suites 1,100,000 lire* 🔲 🔲 🔲 🔲 🔲 🔲 *safe* 🔲 *7am–midnight* 🔲 *Grand Canal* 🔲 *12.30–3pm, 7.30–10.30pm* 🔲 🔲 *10.30am–midnight* 🔲 🔲 🔲 🔲 *7am–10pm* 🔲 🔲 🔲 🔲 🔲 🔲 @ *hmonaco@tin.it*

Sartre and Beauvoir stayed here; now popular with guests from the spheres of culture and politics. Meticulous attention to detail and a beautiful waterside terrace with a wonderful view of Santa Maria della Salute ➡ 90.

Luna Hotel Baglioni (8)
calle Vallaresso, San Marco 1243, 30124
☎ 041 5289840 ➡ 041 5287160

🔲 *San Marco 118 rooms* ●●●●● *7 suites 1,500,000 lire* 🔲 🔲 🔲 🔲 🔲 🔲 🔲 *7am–midnight* 🔲 *safe* 🔲 *Canova* 🔲 *12.30–2.30pm, 7.30–11pm* 🔲 🔲 🔲 *Caffè Baglioni* 🔲 *11am–midnight* 🔲 🔲 🔲 🔲 🔲 🔲 🔲 *banqueting suite* @ *lunavenezia@baglionihotels.com, www.baglionihotels.com*

Possibly Venice's oldest inn: it is said that the Knights Templar used to break their journey here on their way to Jerusalem. True or not, the Baglioni is full of character and equipped with every modern comfort. ★ The Marco Polo room and the Canova Restaurant.

Not forgetting
■ **Albergo Cavalletto e Doge Orseolo (9)** calle fianco la Chiesa del Cavalletto, San Marco 1107, 30124 ☎ 041 5200955 ➡ 041 5238184 *A hotel of understated luxury in a Venetian setting, looking out over a gondola dock.*
■ **Hotel Serenissima (10)** calle Goldoni, San Marco 4486, 30124 ☎ 041 5200011 *Courteous welcome, pleasant atmosphere and attentive service.*

The hotels in the vicinity of Piazza San Marco are often converted historic palazzi, their Rococo décor a reminder of the Most Serene Republic's heyday.

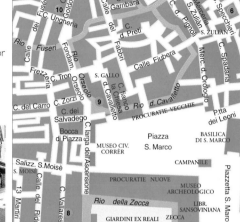

Calle dei Fuseri
C. Ungheria
10
Goldoni
C.d. Garnbara
Calle del Preti
C.d. Pignol
Macorela
S. Zulián
S. ZULIAN
C. d. Specchieri
6
Rio dei Fuseri
Fondam.
C. d. Fabbri
Calle Fiubera
Merc. d. Orologio
C. Spadaria
Frezzeria
C. Tron
Orseolo
S. GALLO
C. d. Chiesa
C. l'Ano
la Chiesa
C. Cavaletto
9
Rio d. Cavaletto
PROCURATIE VECCHIE
C. del Carro
C. Zorzi
C. dei Salvadego
C. larga dell'Ascensione
Bocca di Piazza
Ptta dei Leoni
Piazza S. Marco
BASILICA DI S. MARCO
MUSEO CIV. CORRER
Salizz. S.Moisè
S. MOISÈ
13 Martiri
Calle del Ridotto
C. Valaresso
CAMPANILE
PROCURATIE NUOVE
MUSEO ARCHEOLOGICO
Rio della Zecca
LIBR. SANSOVINIANA
ZECCA
Piazzetta S. Marco
8
GIARDINI EX REALI
CAPIT. DI PORTO
5
7
Fondam. d. Farine

10

9

6

8

8

7

21

➡ Where to stay

Hotel Europa e Regina (11)
calle Barozzi, San Marco 2159, 30124
☎ 041 5200477 ➡ 041 5231533

San Marco, Santa Maria del Giglio **185 rooms** ●●●●● 17 suites 1,516,000 lire 79 000 lire ▯ ▯ ▯ ▯ ▯ ▯ ▯ safe ▯ La Cusina ◷ 12.30–2.30pm, 7.30–10.30pm ▯ ▯ Terrazza Tiepolo ◷ 10am–2pm ▯ ▯ ▯ ▯ ▯ ▯ ▯ banqueting suite ▯ ▯ ▯ @ res075@sheraton.com

The Palazzo Tiepolo, built in the 17th century and altered in the 19th, provides a sumptuous setting for a hotel that has managed to retain the charm and atmosphere of a wealthy, aristocratic residence: fairytale interiors decorated in warm colors, fine furniture, glittering chandeliers made of Murano glass, silk curtains, oriental rugs, and marble everywhere. The bedrooms are spacious and elegant, and equipped with all the comforts expected in a hotel of this category. ★ Small, interconnecting *salotti* and huge public rooms; romantic settings, such as the Terrazza Tiepolo bar and the terrace of the restaurant La Cusina looking out at the palaces along the Grand Canal. In summer, use of a private beach on the Lido ➡ 116.

Hotel La Fenice et des Artistes (12)
campiello della Fenice, San Marco 1936, 30124
☎ 041 5232333 ➡ 041 5203721

Sant'Angelo, San Marco **68 rooms** ●● ▯ ▯ ▯ 8am–9pm ▯ ▯ ▯ ▯ safe ▯ ◷ 8am–9pm ▯ ▯ ▯ ▯ ▯ ▯ banqueting suite ▯ ▯

Divas and conductors from all over the world choose to stay in this hotel for good reasons: it is virtually next door to La Fenice opera house (still undergoing restoration) ➡ 82; it is also quiet, and has plenty of character, especially when it comes to the bedrooms which are furnished in Venetian style. There is no restaurant in the hotel, but the room rates can include meals at Taverna La Fenice ➡ 42.

Santo Stefano (13)
campo Santo Stefano, San Marco 2957, 30124
☎ 041 5200166 ➡ 041 52224460

Accademia, San Samuele **11 rooms** ●● ▯ ▯ ▯ ▯ ▯ ▯ ▯ safe ▯ ▯ ◷ 8am–10pm ▯ ▯ ▯ ▯

This former watchtower from the 14th century with its high, narrow façade, now covered with ivy, once kept the next-door convent under surveillance. The entrance lobby sets the tone: a marriage of modern furnishings and classical architecture. The bedrooms are small, but light and airy, with every comfort. In summer, guests breakfast on the square, just in front of the hotel, behind a screen of greenery, and can watch the spectacle of Campo Santo Stefano, one of the city's liveliest squares.

Not forgetting
■■ **Ala (14)** campo Santa Maria del Giglio, San Marco 2494, 30124 ☎ 041 5208333 ➡ 041 5206390 ●● *Welcoming hotel with comfortable rooms. Terrace with a rooftop view.* ■■ **Locanda Fiorita (15)** campiello Nuovo, San Marco 3457, 30124 ☎ 041 5234754 ➡ 041 5228043 ● *An enchanting place that has just been refurbished. Rather small bedrooms, but a very warm welcome.*

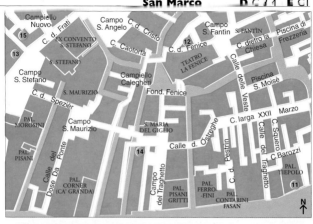

In the area
 Where to stay: ➡ 40 ➡ 44 ➡ 50
➡ **After dark:** ➡ 63 ➡ 66 ➡ 70
➡ **What to see:** ➡ 84 ➡ 94 ➡ 96
➡ **Where to shop:** ➡ 136 ➡ 138 ➡ 140

▶ Where to stay

Locanda Sturion (16)
calle del Storione, San Polo 679, 30125
☎ 041 5236243 ➡ 041 5228378

🚇 *Rialto, San Silvestro* **11 rooms** ●● 🗹 ▭ ⓪ *8am–9.30pm* ◼ ☎ 🛗 Ⅲ
safe 🍸 🍴 *8am–8pm* 🍽 🏳 ♿ ✖ ❄
@ *sturion@tin.it, www.sayville.com/locanda-sturion.html*

As far back as the 13th century, foreign merchants breaking their journey in Venice used to stay here, so the Locanda Sturion can certainly pride itself on a long tradition of hospitality. The location is superb, with breathtaking views over the Grand Canal and the Rialto; an unequalled vantage point for watching the regattas that punctuate Venetian festivals ➡ 76. The bedrooms are very inviting, furnished in typically Venetian style: painted furniture, Murano mirrors and chandeliers, matching drapes and bedspreads. The owners have thought of everything: there is a little library with guides, art books and histories of Venice in several languages, as well as a children's video library. As the Sturion has no restaurant, there is an arrangement with the Bistrot de Venise ➡ 70 entitling guests to a 10% discount.

Pantalon (17)
crosera San Pantalon, Dorsoduro 3491, 30123
☎ 041 710896 ➡ 041 718683

🚇 *San Tomà* **15 rooms** ● 🗹 🗹 ▭ *closed Jan. 10–31* ⓪ *7am–1pm* ◼ ☎ 🛗
Ⅲ *safe* 🍸 🍴 🗓 🍽 ♿ ✖ ❄
@ *hotelpantalon@iol.it, www.venezialberghi.com*

Near the university, in a district mainly frequented by young people. This recently refurbished small hotel has pleasant bedrooms furnished in Venetian style (gilt mirrors, Murano lights) and provided with every comfort. Advantages include the roof garden and solarium, giving guests an opportunity to indulge in a respite from a busy sightseeing program.

Hotel Marconi (18)
riva del Vin, San Polo 729, 30125
☎ 041 5222068 ➡ 041 5229700

🚇 *San Silvestro, Rialto* **26 rooms** ●● 🗹 ▭ ⓪ *7am–8pm* ◼ ☎ 🛗 Ⅲ *safe*
🍸 🍽 ♿ ✖ ❄ @ *info@hotelmarconi.it, www.hotelmarconi.it*

This historic palace, formerly an *osteria* (there used to be many of these in the vicinity, only to be expected on a quay named Riva del Vin), was converted into a hotel in the early 1930s and completely restored in 1991. The public rooms and bedrooms are cozy and romantic, typical of Venetian homes. ★ Attractive terrace overlooking the Grand Canal.

Not forgetting

◼ **San Samuele (19)** salizzada San Samuele, San Marco 3358, 30124
☎ 041 5228045 ● *This small establishment, located in the antiques shop district, is a near neighbor of the house where the painter Veronese lived. Modern, functional furniture in light and airy, well-kept bedrooms. Warm welcome and a friendly atmosphere.*

Tradition and up-to-date comfort, in the heart of Venice, on both sides of the Grand Canal.

In the area
 Where to stay: ➡ 46
▪▪▸ **After dark:** ➡ 62
▸ **What to see:** ➡ 100
▸ **Where to shop:** ➡ 144

Where to stay

Gardena (20)
fondamenta dei Tolentini, Santa Croce 239, 30135
☎ 041 2205000 ➡ 041 2205020

🚋 *Piazzale Roma* **22 rooms** ●● 🔲 🔵 🕐 *7am–11pm* 🔲 📷 📶 🎞 *safe* 🍸
🔲 🔳 🎿 🏋 🗶 📷 🌿 🔵 @ *gardena@tin.it, www.gardenahotels.it*

Totally renovated in 1996, the Gardena occupies an 18th-century palace
with the advantage of being close to the train station (on the opposite side
of the Grand Canal), near Piazzale Roma, in a district where the visitor can
still experience the unpretentious charm of a more modest part of Venice,
relatively unknown to tourists. The bedrooms are comfortable, modern and
given a personal touch with frescos on traditional Venetian themes painted
by young local artists. Breakfast service moves out of doors with the first
rays of spring sunshine. A warm welcome.

Sofitel Venezia (21)
Giardino Papadopoli, Santa Croce 245, 30135
☎ 041 710400 ➡ 041 710394

🚋 *Piazzale Roma* **97 rooms** ●●●●● *5 suites 950,000 lire* 🔲 🔲 🕐 🔲 📷
📶 🎞 🎏 *Papadopoli* 🔵 *12.30–2pm, 7.30–10pm* 🍸 *Salotto Veneziano* 🔲 🔲
🎿 🏋 🗶 🔵 *banqueting suite*

Although it belongs to a chain, this hotel has plenty of character and is
located at the gates of the 19th-century Papadopoli gardens which
form a green curtain, hiding Piazzale Roma, filtering out noise and
pollution and creating an oasis of calm in a rather boisterous district.
The elegant reception rooms, with their luxurious soft furnishings,
provide agreeable retreats for a quiet chat. ★ The dining-room
occupies a very large conservatory, with flourishing plant life, looking
out over the public gardens and is worth a special visit. As befits a
hotel belonging to this chain, the bedrooms have all modern comforts,
and are decorated in the purest Venetian style.

Ai Due Fanali (22)
campo San Simeon Profeta, Santa Croce 946, 30135
☎ 041 718490 ➡ 041 718344

🚋 *Riva di Biasio* **16 rooms** ● 🔵 *20,000 lire* 🔲 🕐 *7–10am* 🔲 📷 📶 🎞
safe 🍸 🔲 🎿 🏋 🗶 📷 🌿 @ *request@aiduefanali.it, www.aiduefanali.com*

This small hotel occupies the former premises of the wool carders'
corporation (Scuola) whose guild church was San Simeon Grande ➡ 100.
The atmosphere is typically Venetian, the bedrooms romantic, with
exposed beams, thick carpeting, painted furniture and bathrooms in
Carrara marble. The hotel also has 4 mini-apartments on the Riva degli
Schiavoni, looking out over St Mark's basin, making it possible to enjoy
hotel service and the privacy of a home-from-home!

Not forgetting

■ **Carlton Executive (23)** fondamenta San Simeon Piccolo, Santa
Croce 578, 30135 ☎ 041 718488 ➡ 041 719061 ●●● *Big hotel belonging to a
chain with extensive and elegant public areas and a Venetian patio.* ■ **Basilea
(24)** calle larga Contarina, Santa Croce 817, 30135 ☎ 041 718477
➡ 041 720851 ●● *Simple bedrooms, but well kept, with Venetian décor.*

In Venice even the hotels belonging to chains have charm and many that are near the train station and Piazzale Roma are quite sophisticated.

20

20

20

22

21

Where to stay

Pensione Seguso (25)
fondamenta Zattere ai Gesuati, Dorsoduro 779, 30123
☎ 041 5286858 ➡ 041 5222340

 Zattere, Accademia **34 rooms** ●● ▣ ▭ *closed Dec.–Feb.* Ⓞ ☎ *safe* ⊞
▦ ⚡ ✦ ⚘

This is something of an institution in Venice, with a delightfully old-fashioned atmosphere, deliberately fostering the quaint charm of early 20th-century *pensioni*. A cozy reading room with wall coverings, fine rugs and inviting leather sofas; the bedrooms are rather faded but comfortable and almost all of them look out over water.

Agli Alboretti (26)
rio terrà Antonio Foscarini, Dorsoduro 884, 30123
☎ 041 5230058 ➡ 041 5210158

 Accademia **19 rooms** ● ▣ ▭ ▦ ⚡ ✦ ☎ *safe* ⊞ *Agli Alboretti* ➡ 48
◷ *12.30–2.30pm, 7.30–10.30pm; closed Wed., lunchtime on Thu., 3 weeks in Aug., 3 weeks in Jan.* @ *alborett@gpnet.it, www.cash.it/alboretti*

Just behind the Accademia Galleries, in a 16th-century palace, is this quiet and secluded hotel. The stylish bedrooms are light and airy; the public rooms, with paneled walls, are on the small side, but very welcoming and with comfortable sofas. In summer breakfast is served in the courtyard in the shade of a pergola.

La Calcina (27)
fondamenta Zattere ai Gesuati, Dorsoduro 780, 30123
☎ 041 5206466 ➡ 041 5227045

▦ *Accademia, Zattere* **29 rooms** ● ▣ ▭ Ⓞ *7am–11pm* ▣ ☎ ▥ *safe* ▾
◿ ▯ ▣ ▦ ⚡ ⚘ ✦ ⚘ @ *la.calcina@iol.it*

This hotel's most famous guest must have been John Ruskin, the art historian, who wrote part of his *Stones of Venice* here. Choose a bedroom that looks out over the Zattere quay, where Venetians love to promenade up and down, with panoramic views toward Giudecca; better still, ask for one with a balcony (but be warned, it will cost more!) ★ The rooftop terrace has a wonderful view of the Redentore church.

Accademia "Villa Maravege" (28)
fondamenta Bollani, Dorsoduro 1058, 30123
☎ 041 5210188 ➡ 041 5239152

▦ *Accademia* **27 rooms** ● ▣ ▭ Ⓞ *7am–1pm, 3.30–9.30pm* ▣ ☎ ▥ *safe*
▾ ◿ ▯ ▦ ⚡ ⚘ ✦ ⚘ @ *pensione.accademia@flashnet.it*

A romantic 17th-century hotel in the heart of the city. In summer, guests have breakfast in the flower-filled garden while they admire the world's most beautiful waterway, the great central 'avenue' of the Grand Canal. Distinctive interior decoration. Essential to book very well ahead.

Not forgetting

■ **Pausania (29)** fondamenta Gherardini, Dorsoduro 2824, 30123
☎ 041 5222083 ➡ 041 5222989 ●● *A typical 14th-century Venetian palace that still has its original well in the courtyard. Attractive bedrooms.*

The Dorsoduro *sestiere* has two facets: one along the Grand Canal, near the Accademia Galleries, and the other on the Zattere, looking toward Giudecca.

In the area
 Where to stay: ➡ 50
➡ **After dark:** ➡ 70
➡ **What to see:** ➡ 100 ➡ 102
➡ **Where to shop:** ➡ 144

➡ Where to stay

Bellini (30)
rio terrà Lista di Spagna, Cannaregio 116/A, 30121
☎ **041 5242488** ➡ **041 715193**

🔲 *Ferrovia* **95 rooms** ●●● 🔲 🔲 🔲 *7–10.30am* 🔲 🔲 🔲 🔲 *safe* 🔲 🔲
🔲 🔲 🔲 🔲 @ *hotel.bellini@boscolo.com, www.boscolohotels.com/bellini*

The unimpressive exterior of this *palazzo* is misleading, concealing a
hotel full of character. ★ Large rooms overlooking the Grand Canal
(some even have a balcony) with coffered ceilings, period furniture,
Murano lights, damask fabrics and an elegant, romantic atmosphere
worthy of the City of the Doges. The public rooms are large, light and
airy, with some fine 19th-century furniture. In warm weather breakfast is
served in the courtyard.

Hesperia (31)
calle Riello, Cannaregio 459, 30121
☎ **041 716001** ➡ **041 715112**

🔲 *Guglie, Ferrovia* **17 rooms** ● 🔲 🔲 *closed 10 days in Dec.* 🔲 *7am–10am*
🔲 🔲 🔲 *safe* 🔲 *Il Melograno* 🔲 *noon–3pm, 7–11pm* 🔲 🔲 🔲 🔲 🔲 🔲
@ *hesperia@shineline.it*

A little *pensione* with painting as its theme: pictures by Nespolo, Schifano
and other modern and contemporary artists hang in the rooms. There is
a family atmosphere, with friendly and attentive service. The bedrooms,
tending toward a modern style, are comfortable and some have views
over the Canareggio canal. Guests can eat at the Melograno, next door.

La Locanda di Orsaria (32)
calle Priuli, Cannaregio 103, 30121
☎ **041 715254** ➡ **041 715433**

🔲 *Ferrovia* **8 rooms** ● 🔲 🔲 🔲 🔲 🔲 🔲 *safe* 🔲 🔲 🔲
@ *orsaria@iol.it, www.venezialberghi.com*

Sheltered from the noise of the Lista di Spagna, the Locanda di Orsaria
has only 8 rooms but all the charm of a family-run *pensione*. Although
small, this is an efficient hotel with the most up-to-date facilities. The
rooms are simple, but welcoming; service has a personal touch, and
nothing is too much trouble to ensure that guests are happy. Generous
breakfast buffet.

Not forgetting

■ **Amadeus (33)** rio terrà Lista di Spagna, Cannaregio 227, 30121
☎ 041 2206000 ➡ 041 2206020 ●●●● *Marble, fountains, gilt mirrors, Murano
crystal: a wealth of opulent furnishings and unrestrained luxury. Breakfast can be
taken in the garden in good weather and there are two restaurants: La Veranda
and Papageno.* ■ **Principe (34)** rio terrà Lista di Spagna, Cannaregio 147,
30121 ☎ 041 2204000 ➡ 041 2204040 ●●● *A large hotel occupying a 15th-
century palace that underwent complete renovation in 1999. Ask for a bedroom at
the back of the building (looking out over the Grand Canal!).* ■ **Zecchini (35)**
rio terrà Lista di Spagna, Cannaregio 152, 30121 ☎ 041 715066
➡ 041 715611 ● *Agreeable and well-run hotel. Modern furniture in rather small
bedrooms and in the communal areas; paintings by contemporary Venetian artists.*

The busy thoroughfare of Lista di Spagna, leading to the train station, is predictably very noisy! But visitors in search of comfort and elegance in this area will not be disappointed.

Where to stay

Giorgione (36)
calle larga dei Proverbi, Cannaregio 4587, 30131
☎ 041 5225810 ➡ 041 5239092

▦ *Ca' d'Oro* **69 rooms** ●●● *13 suites 570,000 lire* 🎏 ▭ 🅞 *7am–noon, 6pm–midnight* ▣ 🕾 🛗 IIII *safe* 🍸 ⤵ ✕ ⚡ ✕ 🚭 ✪
@ giorgione@hotelgiorgione.com, www.hotelgiorgione.it, www.hotelgiorgione.com

An oasis of peace in the heart of Venice, behind the Strada Nuova, the busiest street in the Canareggio *sestiere*. This 15th-century palace was converted into a distinctive hotel more than a century ago. After recent renovation, it has lost none of the atmosphere of an aristocratic residence, and has attained the standards required of a modern 4-star hotel. ★ The tastefully furnished bedrooms are large and romantic, and some have an *altana*, a typically Venetian, small wooden roof-terrace, making it possible to sunbathe in almost total privacy. The courtyard, with its large pool, echoes the atmosphere of the city's *campi* and it is a delight to eat breakfast there in fine weather.

Locanda ai Santi Apostoli (37)
strada Nova, Cannaregio 4391, 30131
☎ 041 5212612 ➡ 041 5212611

▦ *Ca' d'Oro* **9 rooms** ●●● *2 rooms with a view 490,000 lire* 🎏 ▭ *closed Dec. 15–Jan. 15* 🅞 *7.30am–midnight* ▣ 🕾 II▷ 🛗 IIII 🍸 🖵 🐾 ✕ ⚡ ✕

Were it not for the discreet brass plaque by the entrance, it would be easy to miss the Locanda ai Santi Apostoli. Appropriately, given the hotel's name, guests have to ascend heavenward up 3 floors of this old palace to reach the reception area (not as daunting as it may sound, there is an elevator!). Here they can be sure of experiencing the atmosphere that used to exist in an aristocratic house, since the owners treat each and every one of their guests with warmth, attentiveness and tact. The hotel has, moreover, been recently renovated and is now equipped with up-to-date facilities. ★ Two bedrooms look out over the Grand Canal and the Rialto bridge.

Casa Bocassini (38)
calle del Fumo, Cannaregio 5295, 30131
☎ 041 5229892 ➡ 041 5236877

▦ *Fondamenta Nuove* **10 rooms** ● 🎏 ▱ *closed Nov. 15–Dec. 27 and Jan. 10–Feb. 10* 🅞 *8.30–10am* ▣ 🕾 ✕ ⚡ ✪

Another hotel with a family atmosphere where everyone is made to feel very much at home. Nothing is too much trouble for the proprietors who make it their business, simply and without fuss, to ensure that guests have everything they could possibly want. ★ You can picnic in the tiny, enclosed garden court, with flower-covered trellis.

Not forgetting

■ **San Cassiano-Ca' Favretto (39)** calle della Rosa, Santa Croce 2232, 30135 ☎ 041 5241768 ➡ 041 721033 ●● *Looking out over the Grand Canal, facing Ca' d'Oro, this is a long established, traditional hotel with sumptuous décor and furniture. The interiors are typical of a historic palace and the atmosphere is intimate and elegant. Watch out for special offers in the low season!*

36

Courtyards and flower-filled patios, with attractive fountains, lend a certain cachet to those hotels that lack the advantage of a view over the Grand Canal.

36

37

37

39

In the area

- ■▶ **Where to stay:** ➡ 56
- ■▶ **After dark:** ➡ 63 ➡ 64
- ▶ **What to see:** ➡ 78 ➡ 80 ➡112 ➡ 114
- ▶ **Where to shop:** ➡ 132

Where to stay

Bisanzio (40)
calle della Pietà, Castello 3651, 30122
☎ 041 5203100 ➡ 041 52041 14

San Zaccaria **45 rooms** ●●● 🖾 🖃 🔘 🖵 🖾 🖟 🎞 safe 🍸 🖻 🗗 🔏 🖾 ✗ @ www.bisanzio.com

Elegant hotel occupying a 16th-century palace that has been totally restored. Among its advantages: a terrace and a public room leading into a small courtyard, and a mooring pontoon for gondolas and motor-boats. As is often the case in Venice, the bedrooms are not very large, but their parquet floors, painted furniture and the Murano lights make them very pleasant. Generous buffet-style breakfast.

Paganelli (41)
riva degli Schiavoni, Castello 4687, 30122
☎ 041 524324 ➡ 041 5239267

San Zaccaria **22 rooms** ●● 🖾 🖃 🔘 🖵 🖾 🎞 safe 🍸 🖻 🗙 🔏 🖾 🕘 9am–11pm 🔆 @ hotelpag@tin.it, www.gpnet.it/paganelli

There is a modern feel to the entrance lobby; pastel tones and painted, period furniture in the bedrooms, some with views of the lagoon and the island of San Giorgio Maggiore; a room facing onto the quiet little courtyard might be wiser, as the district is quite noisy.

Londra Palace (42)
riva degli Schiavoni, Castello 4171, 30122
☎ 041 5200533 ➡ 041 5225032

San Zaccaria **33 rooms** ●●●●● 20 suites 660,000 lire 🖾 🖃 🔘 🖵 🖾 🖟 🎞 safe 🍴 Do Leoni 🕘 noon–3pm, 7–11pm 🎵 🗗 🍸 🖻 🎵 🖻 🗙 🔏 ✗ ★ 🔆 @ info@hotelondra.it www.hotelondra.it

This small hotel, which dates from 1860, was given a face lift in 1999 by the architect Ettore Morchetti, editor of *A.D*, an Italian interiors magazine. The reception rooms, entrance lobby, restaurant and bar are all decorated in classic style, with trompe l'oeil effects and silk curtains in delicate shades. ★ The bedrooms, all different, are breathtaking: Biedemeier furniture, fine paintings, costly fabrics, marble bathrooms equipped with Jacuzzis… and a panoramic view over St Mark's basin. It is easy to understand how Tchaikovsky was inspired to write his Fourth Symphony here! In summer guests can relax on the rooftop terrace.

Locanda Vivaldi (43)
riva degli Schiavoni, Castello 4150, 30122
☎ 041 2770477 ➡ 041 2770489

San Zaccaria **18 rooms** ●●●● 4 suites 800,000 lire 🖾 🖃 🔘 🖵 🖾 🖟 🎞 safe 🖵 🍸 🎵 🗗 🖻 🗙 🔆 @ info@locandavivaldi.it, www.locandavivaldi.it

A completely new 4-star hotel, situated next door to the Pietà ➡ 63, where the 'red-haired priest', Antonio Vivaldi, was choirmaster and taught the violin. Great care has been taken over the interiors: 18th-century Venetian style predominates, but not to the detriment of modern comfort. ★ Agreeable rooftop terrace where visitors can enjoy an incomparable view over the lagoon.

40

42

43

A short walk from Piazza San Marco, the Riva degli Schiavoni is certainly the busiest pedestrian thoroughfare in Venice. There are a great number of hotels along this quay, to suit every taste and everyone's budget.

42

41

In the early 19th century, people 'discovered' the Lido's fine, sandy beaches ➡ 116; for the aristocracy it became *the* place to be, a summer refuge from Venice's stifling heat. Once Europe's most elegant seaside resort, the Lido has changed a great deal, but the charm of the old days lives on in these elegant luxury hotels. Still *the* place for a unique break!

➡ **Where to stay**

Quattro Fontane (44)
via Quattro Fontane 16, 30126 ☎ 041 5260227 ➡ 041 5260227

Lido, Casinò 🅿 59 rooms ●●●● closed Nov. 15–Apr.1 7.15–10.30am safe Il Platano 12.30–2.30pm, 7.45–10.30pm 11am–midnight 7am–11pm banqueting suite @ info@quattrofontane.com, www.quattrofontane.com

Countrified calm in Venice: the wicker recliners and chairs dotted around the garden set the tone. A short stroll from the beach, this enchanting villa is the prettiest hotel on the Lido: very large *saloni* and public rooms furnished with antiques; secluded alcoves for private conversations, spacious and comfortable bedrooms.

Grand Hotel Excelsior (45)
lungomare Marconi 41, 30126 ☎ 041 5260201 ➡ 041 5267276

Santa Maria Elisabetta 🅿 177 rooms ●●●●● 18 suites 2,300,000 lire closed Dec.–Mar safe Tropicana, La Taverna, La Terrazza Blue Bar, Beach Bar, Pool Bar banqueting suite Ciga Boutique; news-stand; beauty salon @ res077_excelsior@ittsheraton.com, www.luxurycollection.com/excelsiorvenicelido

A fairytale hotel where guests can live in a bygone age of splendor. A Mecca for stars from all over the world during the Mostra. ★ The Excelsior has been transformed: modernity now co-exists harmoniously with the spires and arabesques inspired by Moorish architecture and the early 20th-century interiors. Private beach – the beach huts fetch a higher rental than a hotel bedroom in the center of Venice! – tennis courts, golf and covered riding school.

Grand Hotel Des Bains (46)
lungomare Marconi 17, 30126 ☎ 041 5265921 ➡ 041 5260113

Santa Maria Elisabetta 🅿 191 rooms ●●●●● 1 suite 1,450,000 lire closed Dec.–Mar. Thomas Mann, Liberty, Pagoda banqueting suite beauty salon @ res078_desbains@ittsheraton.com, www.sheraton.com/desbains

For those who enjoy Belle Epoque nostalgia, the Grand Hotel des Bains, immortalized by Visconti in *Death in Venice*, combines elegance, refinement and prestige: immense Art-Deco reception rooms, a majestic veranda where guests can have their meals; spacious and elegant bedrooms furnished with antiques. ★ Three restaurants, two bars, a private beach, an inviting swimming pool in the middle of a garden in bloom, tennis courts.

Villa Mabapa (47)
riviera San Nicolò 16, 30126 ☎ 041 5260590 ➡ 041 5269441

Santa Maria Elisabetta ligne A 🅿 69 rooms ●●● 1 suite 500,000 lire 7am–midnight safe 10am–midnight banqueting suite @ info@villamabapa.com, www.villamabapa.com

When this 1930s villa was converted into a luxury hotel, it retained the atmosphere of a gentleman's home. A profusion of paintings, period furniture and plants. Rooms on the first floor have more character and face the lagoon (the other bedrooms are in an annex). Private beach and landing stage; use of the nearby golf club. Shows and concerts in summer.

Time may seem to have stood still for a century in the luxury hotels on the Lido, but modern comfort has not been forgotten.

S. LAZZARO
DEGLI ARMENI

LAZZARETTO
VECCHIO

Riv. S. Maria

S. Maria Elisabetta

Gran Viale

Via Sandro Gallo

Via Quattro Fontane

Via Zara

Riv. San Nicolo

47

44

Via Dardanelli

46 Marconi

Lungomare Guglielmo

Lungomare
Gabriele D'Annunzio

45

MAR   ADRIATICO

N

45

45

47

44

46

Tourist menus

Beware of tourist menus in fashionable areas, seldom good value for money.
As a rule, it is best to choose fish dishes, prepared with freshly caught
seafood from the lagoon.

Where to eat

Short glossary

Baicoli: crisp, wafer-thin
cookies
Bigoli: outsize, whole wheat
spaghetti, served with a hot
dressing of olive oil, onion
and anchovy
Bisato: full-grown eel
Canoce: mantis shrimp
Caparossoli: small clams
Castraure: baby artichokes
(springtime)
Cicheti: mixed appetizers
Fasioi: white, navy-type
beans
Folpi and folpeti: octopus
in Frito: deep-fried selection
of tiny fish
Moleche: soft-shell crabs
Ombra: a glass of white or
red wine, served at the
counter
Pastissada: the art of using
leftovers (vegetables, pasta,
cured meats, cheese) often
served with polenta
Peoci: mussels
Risi e bisi: thick soup of rice
and peas
Sarde in saor: fried sardines,
marinated in a sauce of
onions, white vinegar, pine
nuts and seedless white
raisins
Schie: very small gray shrimp
Spritz: aperitif made with
white wine, *amaro* and
seltzer water
Zancheti: soles from the
lagoon .

Venetian cuisine

Venetian cooks are masters of the art of preparing fish and crustaceans, drawing on the wealth of the Adriatic. These are accompanied by fresh vegetables from the islands in the lagoon and neighboring mainland. Another local specialty is polenta, which goes with fish or meat, and can be served grilled, fried or in its natural state, with or without a sauce.

47 Restaurants

INDEX BY CUISINE

➡ Where to eat

Gran Caffè Ristorante Quadri (1)
piazza San Marco, San Marco 121, 30124
☎ 041 5222105 ➡ 041 5208041

San Zaccaria **Venetian and classic fish cuisine** ●●●●●
12.15–2pm, 7.15–10.15pm; closed July 25–Aug. 15; Nov.–Mar.: closed Mon @ caffequadri@libero.it

Quadri's is one of three cafés in Piazza San Marco ➡ 64; it is also a restaurant, synonymous, since 1775, with refinement and elegance.
★ A view of the 'finest drawing room in Europe', splendid furniture, Murano glass chandeliers, an intimate and elegant setting: just what is needed to create a magical atmosphere. The cooking here lives up to the décor: red mullet marinated in raspberry vinegar, scallops with saffron, grilled lobster with artichoke sauce and a very good cellar. Their superlative version of baked Alaska is not to be missed.

Ai Mercanti (2)
calle dei Fuseri, San Marco 4346/A, 30124
☎ 041 5238296 ➡ 041 5238296

Rialto **Venetian fish cuisine** ●●● 12.30–2.30pm, 7–10.30pm; closed Sun. and lunchtime Mon

Just a few steps from the legendary Fenice opera house, the appeal of modern décor is surpassed by the charming terrace on a tranquil little square and by the faultless service. The cooking relies on the Venetian repertoire for its fish dishes, but has some surprises with more individual interpretations. Desserts are home-made and the superb sorbets alone would make a visit worthwhile. An interesting wine list.

Antica Carbonera (3)
calle Bembo, San Marco 4648, 30124 ☎ 041 5225479

Rialto **Venetian cuisine** ●● noon–3pm, 7–10pm; closed Thu., Fri. lunchtime, Jan. 7–25 and July15–Aug.15

In the days when coal used to be brought by gondola to the Riva del Carbon nearby, the *gondolieri* used to meet here, in what is apparently one of the oldest inns in Italy. Antica Carbonera has now become an elegant restaurant, the interior resembling a ship's cabin: the tables and partitions were, in fact, salvaged from the yacht of Archduke Rudolph of Hapsburg. The cooking steers clear of gimmickry, transforming the fishermen's daily catch into classic dishes: sardines *in saor*, risotto with cuttlefish ink, poached seafood in its own broth, spider crab, *schie* (tiny gray shrimp) with polenta, calves' liver Venetian style, or, more simply, broiled fish.

Not forgetting

■ **Al Graspo de Ua (4)**, campo San Bartolomio, San Marco 5094, 30124 ☎ 041 5200150 ➡ 041 5233917 ●●●● noon–3pm, 7–11pm; closed Mon. *A typically Venetian eating place where diners can enjoy scampi with artichoke, spaghettini Dalmatian style, turbot with tiny olives, casseroled eel... and very good wines from the Veneto region.* ■ **Al Colombo (5)**, corte Teatro, San Marco 4619, 30124 ☎ 041 5222627 ➡ 041 5237498 ●●● noon–midnight. *Founded in the 18th century, this restaurant's forte is freshly caught fish and home-made pasta.*

Where to eat

Taverna La Fenice (6)
campiello della Fenice, San Marco 1936, 30124
☎ 041 5223856 ➡ 041 5237866

▨ *Sant'Angelo* **Venetian and classic cuisine** ▣ ●●●● ▱ ❚❚ ◷ *noon–3pm, 7–11pm; closed Sun.* ▨ ♫ ▽ @ *www.tavernalafenice.com*

Paneled walls, fine furniture, period glass and soft lighting conjure up echoes of the great opera house, which has provided this restaurant with most of its clientele for over a century. The most cooking pays homage to the Venetian tradition, with many variations on the themes of fish and wild mushrooms, relying on the well-stocked cellar to offer a wine suited to each dish. During cold winter weekends, a pianist brings an extra spark of warmth to the atmosphere.

Harry's Bar (7)
calle Vallaresso, San Marco 1323, 30124
☎ 041 5285777 ➡ 041 5208822

▨ *San Marco* **Venetian and classic cuisine** ▣ ●●●●● ▱ ❚❚ ◷ *11.30am–3pm, 7–10pm* ▥ ▽ ▨ @ *harrys@pop.gpnet.it, www.cipriani.com*

A real institution in Venice, where Hemingway was a regular. Harry's Bar is worth a special visit for its atmosphere, aperitifs and service rather than for its cooking: meals are extremely expensive. Excellent wines, especially the champagnes, on which a number of the cocktails are based.

Antico Martini (8)
campo San Fantin, San Marco 1983, 30124
☎ 041 5237027 ➡ 041 5289857

▨ *San Marco, Santa Maria del Giglio* **Venetian and classic fish cuisine** ▣ ●●●●● ▱ ❚❚ ◷ *noon–2.30pm, 7–11.45pm; closed lunchtime Tue. and Wed.* ▥ ▨ ▽ @ *info@anticomartini.com, www.anticomartini.com*

When the Teatro La Fenice first opened in the 18th century, Antico Martini was just a café: subsequently, it became the haunt of intellectuals, singers, actors and conductors from the opera house. Its appeal lies in its typically Venetian setting and atmosphere as well as its cooking, equally at home with dishes that are native to the lagoon and with more adventurous creations. Well-stocked cellar and faultless service.

La Caravella (9)
calle larga XXII Marzo, San Marco 2397, 30124
☎ 041 5208901-041 5208938 ➡ 041 5207131

▨ *San Marco, Santa Maria del Giglio* **Venetian and classic cuisine** ●●●●● ▱ ❚❚ ◷ *noon–3pm, 7–11pm* ▥ ▽ ▨ @ *www.hotelsaturnia.it/caravella/caravel.htm*

The décor suggests a luxurious sailing ship's cabin. The cooking also speaks volumes about the sea and the lagoon. In summer, diners eat by candlelight in the flowery little courtyard.

Not forgetting
■ **Alla Borsa (10)** calle delle Veste, San Marco 2018, 30124 ☎ 041 5235434 ➡ 041 5200021 ●●● ◷ *noon–11pm Seafood and dishes from the Veneto hinterland.*

The *Bellini* was invented at Harry's Bar: the main ingredients are peach juice and Prosecco wine.

In the area

 Where to stay: ➠ 24 ➠ 32
After dark: ➠ 66
What to see: ➠ 94
Where to shop: ➠ 136 ➠ 140

Where to eat

Trattoria alla Madonna (11)
calle della Madonna, San Polo 594, 30125
☎ 041 5223824 ➠ 041 5210167

⬚ *Rialto, San Silvestro* **Venetian seafood cuisine** ●● ▭ ◷ *noon–3pm, 7–10.30pm; closed Wed., Jan. and Aug. 15–31* ▥

The atmosphere here is friendly, convivial and lively, the service courteous and attentive. The cooking places tremendous importance on freshly caught fish (the seafood display near the entrance is the best possible proof of this) prepared with the utmost faithfulness to Venetian tradition. Since the menu has no place for pointless experimentation, this is the place to savor genuine fare: spider crab served in its shell, superlative *scampi* or clam risotto, cuttlefish Venetian style and an unforgettable mixed baby fish fry. Wonderful mixed seafood platter.

Antica Ostaria Ruga Rialto (12)
calle del Storione, San Polo 629, 30125
☎ 041 5211243 ➠ 041 2419946

⬚ *San Silvestro, Rialto* **Venetian cuisine** ◧ ● ▭ ◷ *10am–3pm, 6–11pm; closed Mon. and Jan.* ▱ ▼

Despite its location in the middle of the Rialto *sestiere*, a very busy tourist district, this establishment has managed to maintain the atmosphere of an old Venetian *osteria* while keeping up with changing tastes. There is a warm welcome; the long counter is stacked with both traditional and inventive *cicheti* (boiled meat salad (*nerveti*), little gray shrimp (*schie*), *pasta e fasioi*…), to be accompanied, of course, by an *ombra* when it is time for an aperitif. More substantial dishes are also available, and change from day to day.

Ostaria Sopra al Ponte (13)
campo delle Beccarie
San Polo 1588, 30125 ☎ 041 718208

⬚ *San Silvestro, Rialto, San Stae* **Venetian seafood cuisine** ◧ ● ▭ ▨ ◷ *8am–3pm, 6–10pm; summer: closed Sun. and Aug. 15–31; winter: closed Mon.* ▥ ▱ ▼

Two brothers, each with his wife to help him, run this typical Venetian *osteria*. None of the traditional features is missing: exposed beams, a long counter, old wooden tables, Venetian prints hanging on the walls, paper table napkins, an unpretentious, friendly atmosphere and a menu based solely on fish: spaghetti comes with *caparossoli* (Venetian clams), or with mussels or *scampi* or home-made fresh tomato sauce; fried or broiled fish; stockfish (dried cod), creamed, or in tomato sauce or Vicenza style. Weekend cooking is more elaborate, giving star billing to red mullet or mantis shrimps. Good choice of wines with about fifty local varieties.

Not forgetting

■ **Poste Vece (14)** Pescaria, San Polo 1608, 30125 ☎ 041 721822 ●●●
◷ *noon–2.45pm, 7–10.15pm; closed Tue. Regional cooking with seafood specialties (baked turbot; Chef's special sea bream; black cuttlefish ink tagliolini with crab; rock lobster). An elegant, sophisticated restaurant.*

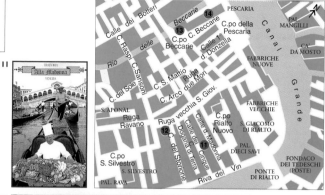

13

Venetian gastronomy owes more to the San Polo *sestiere* than any other.

13

14

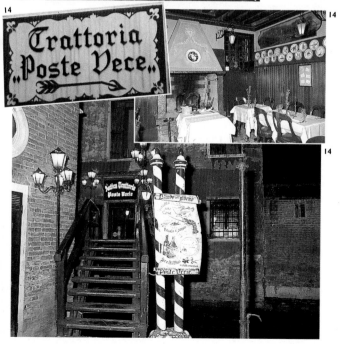

14

14

➡ Where to eat

Da Ignazio (15)
calle Saoneri, San Polo 2749, 30125 ☎ 041 5234852 ➡ 041 2448546

San Tomà **Venetian cuisine** ●● ◻ 🕓 noon–3pm, 7–10pm; closed Sat. and Dec. 24–Jan. 10, Feb. 20–27, 15 days in Aug.

An agreeable place where meals can be served in the open air. After a first course of traditional seafood *cicheti*, choose a classic dish from the lagoon's repertoire or, for those who prefer meat, calves' liver, ossobuco…

Osteria da Fiore (16)
calle dello Scaleter, San Polo 2202/A, 30125
☎ 041 721308 ➡ 041 721343

San Tomà, San Stae **Modern cuisine based on fish** ●●●●●
◻ 🕓 12.30–2.30pm, 7.30–10.30pm; closed Sun., Mon., 3 weeks in Aug., Dec. 25–Jan. 15 ||| 🔁 🍷 🎦 @ www.dafiore.com

Everyone seems to agree that some of the best cooking in Europe is to be found here. The atmosphere is welcoming and the décor elegant; superb raw materials are cooked without affectation, bringing traditional recipes up to date, highlighting natural flavors. Excellent service; extensive wine list. Look out for: deep-fried baby fish and vegetables, risottos, seafood ravioli, deep-fried pieces of sole and zucchini, fillet of sea bass flavored with balsamic vinegar. Leave room for the mouthwatering desserts.

La Zucca (17)
ramo del Megio, Santa Croce 1762, 30135 ☎ 041 5241570

San Stae **Creative cuisine** ● ◻ 🕓 12.30–3pm, 7–10.30pm; closed Sun., week of Aug. 15, from Christmas through New Year's Day 🔁

A menu that does wonders with pumpkin and other produce from the vegetable garden: pumpkin and ricotta pie, guinea fowl with mushrooms and polenta, beef with chickpeas or with couscous, sweet chestnut mousse with *baicoli*. One of the rare places in Venice where excellence is easily affordable; space for only 25!

Osteria al Ponte "La Patatina" (18)
calle Saoneri, San Polo 2741, 30125 ☎ 041 5237238

San Tomà **Venetian cuisine** ● ◻ 🕓 9.30am–2.30pm, 4.30–9pm; closed Sun. ||| 🔁 🍷 🎦 @ macigarbin@libero.it

Working people, gondoliers and students come here. Some hot fish dishes at lunchtime but *cicheti* are the main attraction (sardines *in saor*, home-cured variety meats with polenta, little meat balls, vegetables in crisp, light batter, and the house specialty: sautéed or deep-fried potatoes *en brochette*). Bottled wines or carafes of house wine.

Not forgetting

■ **Vivaldi (19)** calle della Madonnetta, San Polo 1457, 30125 ☎ 041 5238185 ● 🕓 11am–3pm, 7–11pm; closed Sun. in summer *Very wide variety of* cicheti *to eat at the counter or take out.* ■ **Antica Besseta (20)** salizzada Ca' Zusto, Santa Croce 1395, 30135 ☎ 041 721687 ●●●●● 🕓 noon–2pm, 7–10pm; closed lunchtime Tue. and Wed. *Typical osteria with* cicheti *and traditional dishes.*

In the vicinity of Piazza San Marco, it is increasingly difficult to find genuine Venetian *osterie*; these are gradually replaced by 'tourist restaurants'.

In the area

 Where to stay: ➡ 28
After dark: ➡ 62 ➡ 68 ➡ 70
What to see: ➡ 86 ➡ 88 ➡ 90
Where to shop: ➡ 142

Where to eat

Ai Gondolieri (21)
fondamenta Zorzi Bragadin, Dorsoduro 366, 30123
☎ 041 5286396 ➡ 041 5210075

▦ Accademia, Zattere **Venetian cuisine** ▣ ●●●● ▤ ◷ *noon–3pm, 7–10pm; closed Tue.* Ⅲ ⬩ ▼ @ *aigond@gpnet.it, www.aigondolieri.com*

Giovanni Trevisan has a culinary philosophy that goes against the flow: despite the proximity of the Adriatic sea, he serves only meat and poultry dishes skillfully complemented by fresh, seasonal vegetables. Although his cooking reflects the influence of Venetian tradition, he has achieved his own, very personal interpretation of the 'classics': warm smoked duck breast salad with balsamic vinegar, savory polenta cake with diced *pancetta* and mushrooms, duck with apple compote and home-made onion relish and, of course, Venetian style calves' liver. There is an excellent wine list, as well as a mouthwatering cheese board, and a very good selection of desserts.

Agli Alboretti (22)
rio terrà Antonio Foscarini, Dorsoduro 883, 30123
☎ 041 5230058 ➡ 041 5210158

▦ Accademia, Zattere **Modern cuisine** ▣ ●●● ▤ ◷ *12.30–2.30pm, 7.30–10.30pm; closed lunchtime Wed., Thu., Aug. and Jan.* ⬩ ▼ @ *alborett@gpnet.it, www.cash.it/alboretti*

This hotel restaurant (Agli Alboretti ➡ 28) has several pleasant surprises in store: a smiling welcome, a tranquil and friendly atmosphere and, in summer, the chance to eat outside under the shade of a pergola. The fine cooking includes both traditional and more creative fish and meat dishes. The menu changes each month to reflect the passing seasons: autumn's arrival can bring with it a gratin of pumpkin with *amaretti* and coriander, warm terrine of salmon layered with wild fennel and orange slices in puff pastry, braised porcini mushrooms and sweet chestnuts, fish or vegetable risottos, monkfish with fresh herbs… Choose from more than 300 wines.

Osteria ai quattro ferri (23)
campo San Barnaba, Dorsoduro 2754/B, 30123 ☎ 041 5206978

▦ Ca' Rezzonico, San Tomà, Accademia **Venetian cuisine** ● ▤ ◷ *11am–3pm, 6.30pm–midnight; closed Sun.* ⬩ ▼

A typical *osteria* providing traditional *cicheti* and lovingly prepared Venetian dishes using the best fresh ingredients bought daily from the markets. Specialties well worth trying include cream of leek soup; spaghetti with clams or with home-made, fresh tomato sauce, and the broiled fish.

Not forgetting

■ **Da Sandro (24)** calle lunga San Barnaba, Dorsoduro 2753, 30123 ☎ 041 5230531 ● ◷ *12.15–2.30pm, 7.15–9.30pm; closed Sun. and Mon. Dishes from Venice and the Veneto region, served at table or eaten at the counter.*
■ **Antica Locanda Montin (25)** fondamenta delle Romite, Dorsoduro 1147, 30123 ☎ 041 5227151 ➡ 041 5200255 ●● ◷ *12.30–2pm, 7.30–10pm; closed Tue. evening and Wed. Belonging to the pensione of the same name, this restaurant is particularly agreeable in summer for meals outside, under the climber-smothered pergola.*

Hotel restaurants tend to have an indifferent reputation; Agli Alboretti is an exception, with its refreshingly relaxed atmosphere, a warm welcome and good cooking.

In the area

 Where to stay: ➡ 19 ➡ 30

 After dark: ➡ 62 ➡ 66 ➡ 70

What to see: ➡ 102 ➡ 104

Where to shop: ➡ 144

Where to eat

Sahara (26)

fondamenta della Misericordia, Cannaregio 2519, 30121
☎ 041 721077 ➡ 041 715977

San Marcuola, Madonna dell'Orto **Syrian cuisine** 🔲 ● ▤ 🕐 10.30am–2.30pm, 7pm–2am; closed Mon. and Mon.–Thu. in Nov. ▥ ↙ 🎵

For those who feel like a change from the local, fish-based cuisine: an unusual restaurant in a very picturesque corner of Venice, one of the few in the city serving non-Italian food. The very likeable couple in charge serve food from Syria (the owner's native land) and other Middle Eastern dishes with tempting, exotic names: *baba ghannoug* (eggplant caviar and sesame seed paste), *shawarma* (broiled marinated lamb cutlets), *kafta* (kebabs of finely chopped meat flavored with parsley, onion and spices) and, of course, meat and vegetable couscous.
★ Belly dancing performances on Friday and Saturday nights.

Bacco (27)

fondamenta delle Cappuccine, Cannaregio 3054, 30121
☎ 041 71749-041 721415

San Marcuola, Guglie **Venetian cuisine** ●● ▤ 🕐 noon–2pm, 7–10pm; closed Mon., 15 days in Jan., 15 days in Aug. ↙ ▼

A walk along the entire length of this *fondamenta*, opposite the Ghetto, leads to an authentic part of Venice, away from the well-trodden tourist itineraries. A district of craftsmen's workshops and *bacari*: very unpretentious wine bars where it is the custom to eat several *cicheti* while sipping an *ombra*. Bacco is just such a place, with the warm, inviting atmosphere typical of old-fashioned *osterie* and large wooden tables. If you arrive early, you will probably find the owner still busy preparing the *cicheti*, a guarantee of their freshness! You can also enjoy Venetian dishes with no frills: *taglioni* with spider crab; black spaghetti made with cuttlefish ink; hot, savory *bigoli*; casseroled eel.

Antica Mola (28)

fondamenta degli Ormesini, Cannaregio 2800, 30121 ☎ 041 717492

San Marcuola, Guglie **Venetian cuisine** 🔲 ● ▤ 🕐 noon–midnight; closed Wed. in low season and Aug. ▼

Situated on a canal, Antica Mola's does not look promising, having all the outward appearance of a tourist restaurant. But the cooking makes a visit well worthwhile, especially as prices are reasonable for such high quality: the predominantly Venetian clientele knows what it is about. The menu offers fish specialties such as *sarde in saor*, seafood risotto, *gnochetti* with spider crab, cuttlefish, as well as meat and poultry dishes, including excellent calves' liver with polenta. In fine weather, tables are also set up in the garden.

Not forgetting

■ **Osteria Anice Stellato (29)** fondamenta della Sensa, Cannaregio 3272, 30121 ☎ 041 720744 ●● 🕐 12.30–2.30pm, 7.30–10.30pm; closed Mon. *Come here for a sustaining snack or for a later, more substantial meal (mussels, stuffed squid, carpacci and baked fish).*

To round off the meal at the very welcoming Sahara, try their exotic specialty of 'white coffee', flavored with oriental spices.

In the area
➡️ **Where to stay:** ➡ 32
➡️ **After dark:** ➡ 62 ➡ 68 ➡ 70
➡️ **What to see:** ➡ 94 ➡ 106 ➡ 108
➡️ **Where to shop:** ➡ 140

➡️ Where to eat

Vini da Gigio (30)
fondamenta della Chiesa, Cannaregio 3628, 30131
☎ 041 5285140 ➡ 041 5228597

🔲 *Ca d'Oro, San Marcuola* **Venetian fish cuisine** 🔶 ●● ▭
🕐 *noon–2.30pm, 7.30–10.30pm; closed Mon., 15 days in Jan. and Aug.* ◪

The recipe for success here is high quality food at reasonable prices (possibly the best value in Venice) and an exceptional wine list offering top French and Italian vintages as well as American, Australian and South African wines. The cooking relies on seafood from the lagoon (soft shell crabs, schie, broiled eels). Attentive service.

Fiaschetteria Toscana (31)
salizzada San Giovanni Crisostomo, Cannaregio 5719, 30131
☎ 041 5285281 ➡ 041 5285521

🔲 *Rialto* **Venetian cuisine** 🔶 ●●● ▭ 🕐 *12.30–2.30pm, 7.30–10.30pm; closed Mon. lunch, Tue., May 15–July15* ▥

Despite having been named in honor of Florence and its surrounding region, this restaurant keeps faith with the Venetian tradition. Some excellent cured meats and sausages from Tuscany are, however, served here. Freshly caught fish; seasonal produce chosen with the greatest care; faultless service, an appetizing cheese board, and a good choice of wines. The desserts are absolutely delicious.

Ca' d'Oro – Alla Vedova (32)
strada Nova, Cannaregio 3912, 30131 ☎ 041 5285324

🔲 *Ca' d'Oro* **Venetian cuisine** ● ▭ 🔶 🕐 *11.30am–2.30pm, 6.30–10.30pm; closed Thu., lunchtime Sun., late July and Aug.* ◪ ▯

The mother of the present owners, the original *vedova* (widow) made this wine bar a success and it is worth a special visit for the countless *cicheti* on display at the counter: all sorts of bite-sized snacks including deep-fried vegetables, creamed stockfish, shrimp brochettes and cuttlefish. The atmosphere and décor are reminiscent of an old inn, with wood everywhere, soft lights, copper casserole dishes, engravings on the walls and long, wooden tables. Advisable to make reservations ahead.

Tre Spiedi B.E.S. (33)
salizzada San Canziano, Cannaregio 5906, 30131 ☎ 041 520835

🔲 *Rialto, Ca' d'Oro* **Venetian cooking** ● ▭ 🕐 *noon–2.30pm, 7–9.30pm; closed Sun. evening, Mon., last week July–Aug.10, Christmas and New Year's Day* ▥

This rustic style *trattoria* has a mainly Venetian clientele. The atmosphere is lighthearted, serving simple, well-cooked dishes such as fish risotto, grilled squid and shrimp. Be prepared for a wait: no reservations accepted for this popular place.

Not forgetting
■ **La Cantina (34)** strada Nova, Cannaregio 3689, 30131 ☎ 041 5228258 ➡ 041 9360122 ● 🕐 *8.30am–9pm; closed Sun. in low season. A choice of 70 different wines; a short menu with classic Venetian dishes; very wide selection of cured meats and sausages, and cheeses.*

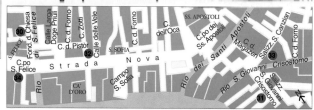

Venetian restaurants make it a point of honor to have a good wine list; Vini da Gigio can offer an amazingly wide choice of wines from all over the world.

30

FIASCHETTERIA TOSCANA

Ristorante in Venezia

31

32

32

34

34

In the area

- **Where to stay:** ➡ 32
- **After dark:** ➡ 62 ➡ 68
- **What to see:** ➡ 78 ➡ 108 ➡ 110
- **Where to shop:** ➡ 132

➡ **Where to eat**

Antico Pignolo (35)
calle Specchieri, San Marco 451, 30124
☎ 041 5228123 ➡ 041 5209007

▨ Rialto, San Marco **International cuisine, specializing in fish** ◨ ●●●●●
▤ ▮▮ ▣ noon–2.30pm, 7–10.30pm ▥ ⬛ ⬛ ⬛

A first-class restaurant with an atmosphere of friendliness and professionalism. It is noted for the absolute freshness of its fish and crustaceans (demonstrated by the presence of crawfish and lobsters swimming about in a tank) and faultless, top-notch service, complemented by a choice of some 900 wines from the exceptional cellar. A particularity worth noting: there are two versions of each dish, with or without truffles.

Alle Testiere (36)
calle Mondo Nuovo, Castello 5801, 30122
☎ 041 5227220 ➡ 041 5227220

▨ Rialto **Venetian cuisine** ●●● ▤ ▣ 11am–3pm, 6–10pm; closed Sun., July 27–Aug. 28, Dec. 23–Jan. 10.

The saying that small is beautiful certainly applies here: the restaurant is tiny, and the cooking bears witness to the chef's skill and expertise, with an ability to make the most of recipes from the Venetian gastronomic repertoire and to select excellent raw materials (*schie* with white polenta, *folpeti* with sauce, spaghettini with squid, roast turbot with Treviso endive). As in any self-respecting *osteria*, there is a good selection of *cicheti*. It would be a shame to miss out on the desserts. The décor is unusual: wrought-iron bedheads (hence *testiere*) attached to the walls or used as shelf supports for glasses and as wine racks.

Osteria alla Frasca (37)

corte Carità, Cannaregio 5176, 30131 ☎ 041 5285433

▨ Fondamenta Nuove **Venetian cuisine** ● ▤ ▣ 9am–2.30pm, 6–9.30pm; summer: closed Sun. lunch and week of Aug.15; winter: closed Sun. evening and Jan. ⬛ ⬛

This was once Titian's studio, where he kept his canvases and his paints. It is, however, totally off the tourist track, so entails a special visit. The premises are so small that meals are served outside all year round, under an awning (at the first hint of chilliness, heating is provided). The cooking does, of course, follow regional tradition, taking equal care over seafood specialties (spaghetti with clams, cuttlefish with polenta) and dishes from the Veneto hinterland. There is, of course, a selection of *cicheti* for a quick lunch.

Not forgetting

■ **Al Portego (38)** calle della Malvasia, Castello 6014, 30122
☎ 041 5229038 ● ▣ 9.30am–10pm; closed Sun. *Good selection of* cicheti: *rissoles, fried vegetables in batter,* crostini *– and some traditional dishes.*
■ **Osteria da Alberto (39)** calle larga Giacinto Gallina, Cannaregio 5401, 30131 ☎ 041 5238153 ● ▣ 11am–2.30pm, 6–9.30pm, closed Sun. *All the Venetian specialties and some original creations, with a predilection for fish.*

36

38

38

36

35

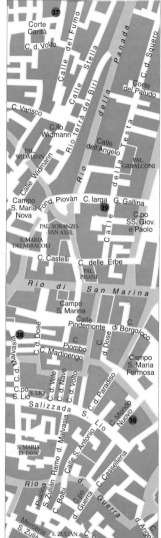

37

55

In the area
- **Where to stay:** ➡ 18 ➡ 34
- **After dark:** ➡ 63
- **What to see:** ➡ 80 ➡ 112 ➡ 114
- **Where to shop:** ➡ 132

Where to eat

Da Remigio (40)
salizzada dei Greci, Castello 3416, 30122
☎ 041 5230089 ➡ 041 2417828

San Zaccaria, Arsenale **Venetian cuisine** ●●● ▭ 🍴 🕐 *12.30–2.30pm, 7.30–10pm; closed Mon. evening, Tue., July 20–Aug.10, Dec. 20–Jan. 25* ▥

There is no hope of going straight to a table without a reservation: there is always a line outside this restaurant, proof of good food. Customers need to wait patiently (not least because the service is also rather slow), perhaps while sipping a *spritz* at the bar and studying the menu. In common with all *trattorie* patronized by Venetians, this one serves *sarde in saor*, raw clams, cooked octopus and shrimp as appetizers, and a main course of broiled fish, freshly caught in the lagoon. The city's inhabitants rub shoulders with tourists here.

Al Covo (41)
calle Crosera, Castello 3968, 30122
☎ 041 5223812 ➡ 041 5223812

San Zaccaria, Arsenale **Venetian cuisine** ●●●● ▤ 🍴 🕐 *noon–2pm, 8–10pm; closed Wed., Thu., Dec. 18–Jan. 18, 10 days in Aug.* ▨

One of the best finds in Venice, with a unique atmosphere. Front of house, Dianne, an American by birth, takes care of the clientele – and it goes without saying that English speakers will have no communication problem here. In the kitchen Cesare takes pride in creating light, digestible dishes with lagoon fish (served with young, strictly seasonal, vegetables): *carpaccio* of sea bream; baked scallops; poached seafood with mixed vegetables, *bigoli* with hot dressing. Dianne makes the desserts and their transatlantic flavor provides a pleasantly surprising finish to an otherwise typically Venetian menu.

Corte Sconta (42)
calle del Prestin, Castello 3886, 30122
☎ 041 5227024 ➡ 041 5227513

Arsenale, San Zaccaria **Venetian cuisine** ●●● ▤ 🕐 *11am–3.30pm, 6–10pm; closed Sun., Mon., July 18–Aug.18, Jan. 8–Feb.8.* ▨

Combine equal parts of good cooking, reasonable prices and agreeable service: this is Corte Sconta's recipe for success. The atmosphere is lively, almost noisy, since the restaurant is always full, which is why the owners have had to resort to two sittings. There is such a wide variety of appetizers (including spider crabs, *caparossoli* and delicious sardines *in saor*) that they make a meal in themselves! The main courses (spaghetti with clams or with cuttlefish ink, 'risotto al go' (a type of eel) *gnocchetti* with lobster, grilled red mullet with a squeeze of fresh lemon) are, quite simply, delicious. A careful perusal of the list of Venetian specialties ➡ 38 before eating here is advisable, as only the local dialect is spoken.

Not forgetting

■ **Rivetta (43)** ponte San Provolo, Castello 4625, 30122 ☎ 041 5287302 ●● 🕐 *11am–10pm; closed Mon. This eating house is always busy and, consequently, rather noisy, serving very good food. As always, there is a choice of cicheti at the counter, as well as hot dishes served at table.*

A successful marriage of Italian and American flair at the Covo: traditional Venetian dishes and home-made American desserts.

➡ Where to eat

Locanda Cipriani (44)
piazza San Fosca 29, Torcello, 30012 ☎ 041 730150 ➡ 041 735433

📺 Torcello **Classic fish cuisine** ●●●●● 🖬 📗 🕐 *noon–3pm; 7–10pm; closed Tue., Jan. 6–Feb. 12* 🏨 ⬆ 🔳 🔲 @ *info@locandacipriani.com, www.locandacipriani.com*

No sooner has the visitor set foot on Torcello ➡ 116, third largest of the lagoon's islands, than its magic gets to work. It is easy to understand why Hemingway spent a lot of time here, putting the finishing touches to his novel *Across the River and Into the Trees*. Enchantment is guaranteed, by the setting (particularly entrancing when the roses are in bloom, for a meal under the awning), by the view (over the lagoon) and by the cooking, which concentrates on seafood. Among the most successful dishes are seafood salad, risotto Torcello style, with seasonal vegetables, and baked John Dory, garnished with fresh tomatoes and capers. A 'patriotic' wine list, with some sixty Italian wines to choose from.
★ There are a limited number of bedrooms available for a very romantic stay, but it is essential to book a long time ahead! A motor-boat shuttle service runs from San Marco to Torcello at lunchtime, from Friday through Sunday.

Trattoria Laguna (45)
**via Pordelio 444, Cavallino, 30013
☎ 041 968058 ➡ 041 698058**

📺 Punta Sabbioni **Venetian fish cuisine** ●●● 🖬 🕐 *12.30–2pm, 7–10.30pm; closed Thu., June 15–Sep.15: Thu. lunchtime, Jan. 1–Feb. 8.* 🏨 🔲

For twenty-five years, the same family has lovingly nurtured this restaurant, situated on a tiny island in the middle of the lagoon.

The fare at their welcoming and traditional *trattoria* betrays a passion for freshly caught fish, broiled and served with tender young vegetables from their garden. Among the outstanding dishes are: risotto al go (a type of eel, from the lagoon), potato *gnocchi* with smoked eel, baked turbot, broiled eel and, of course, the desserts, including an unusual one made with Treviso red endives.

Al Gatto nero - da Ruggero (46)
fondamenta della Giudecca 88, Burano, 30012 ☎ 041 730120

Mazzorbo **Venetian creative cuisine** 🎨 ●● 🍴 🕓 *noon–3pm, 7–9pm; closed Mon. and May and Nov. (variable)* Ⅲ 🎫 🍷 @ www.gattonero.com

If Venetians have no hesitation about making a special boat trip to Burano ➡ 116, the lacemaking island, just to eat at Ruggero's, the food must be good! The walls of the restaurant's very large room are covered with paintings (the owner's passion), there is a terrace beside the canal and the table settings are beautiful. Service is attentive and courteous, the menu an inventory of the specialties of the lagoon, cooked with scrupulous respect for tradition: risotto alla buranella (with eels), *gnochetti* with spider crab, *tagliolini* with *scampi* or porcini mushrooms, broiled seafood, a *grande fritto misto* (a selection of 8 varieties of deep-fried seafood in batter); polenta with Venice's *schie* (little gray shrimp) and, in season, game. Mooring usually available for those who come by boat.

Not forgetting

🏠 **Busa alla Torre (47)** campo Santo Stefano 3, Murano, 30141
☎ 041 739662 ➡ 041 739662 ●● 🕓 11.30am–4pm *At the far end of the Fondamenta dei Vetrai, a traditional* trattoria, *its cooking typical of the lagoon.*

Cinema, theater and dance

As well as its world-famous art exhibition ➡ 114, the Biennale organizes a movie festival (la Mostra) on the Lido ➡ 116 in August/September, and a number of musical, dance and theatrical events.

La Biennale di Venezia ☎ 041 5218711 @ www.labiennale.org

➤ After dark

'Bacari'

The word *bacaro* – a wine bar – is said to derive from the Latin *bacchari*: to celebrate the feast of Bacchus. Friends meet here to drink an *ombra* (shadow/shade). This strange expression for a glass of wine is supposed to have originated when wine was sold from the barrel in Piazza San Marco. As the day wore on, trestles, demijohns and barrels were moved around to keep the wine cool in the shadow of the bell-tower.

Venice by night

Venetians traditionally go to bed early, as you will realize if you are out after 10pm. However, the trend seems to be changing, with many establishments remaining open until late, especially around the Campo Santa Margherita, where students traditionally gather.

What's on this evening?
To find out all about the city's cultural events – concerts, plays, movies, exhibitions, markets – buy a copy of the invaluable *Venezia News*. It is published in Italian and English versions (4,000 lire).

24
Nights out

Dancing
For those who enjoy painting the town red, here are the addresses of two popular discos: **Casanova Disco Cafè** *rio Terrà Lista di Spagna, Cannaregio 158/A, 30121* ☎ *041 2750199* and **Pachuka** *via Spiaggia San Nicolò, Lido* ☎ *041 2420020*.

Gambling
For those who cannot resist a little flutter, there is just one place to go: the **municipal casino** *campiello Vendramin, Cannaregio 2040, 30121* ☎ *041 5297111* ➠ *106*; in summer, it transfers to the Lido, to the Lungomare Marconi ➠ *116*.

There is no shortage of concerts and plays in the city of Vivaldi and Goldoni. The orchestra of the Fenice Opera House carries on with its seasons in the pavilion erected on Tronchetto, while first-rate ensembles give concerts all the year round and plucky little theater companies stage some excellent productions.

After dark

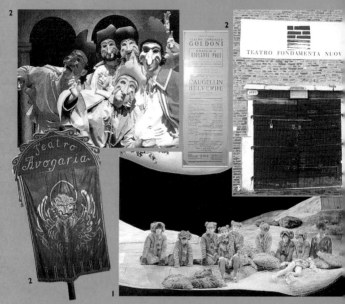

PalaFenice (1)
Isola Nuova del Tronchetto, 30100 ☎ 041 5204010 ➡ 041 786580

🚟 Tronchetto *opera house* 🍴 🕐 *times vary; closed Mon.* ● *30,000–80,000 lire* 📠 📺 🖨 @ *www.tin.it/fenice, fenice@interbusiness.it. Ticket office: campo San Fantin, San Marco 1965 ☎ 041 786520 and Cassa di Risparmio, campo San Luca, San Marco ☎ 041 5210161 🕐 8.30am–1.30pm*

The Palafenice is the large pavilion that provides a temporary home for productions normally staged at La Fenice which has taken longer than expected to rise from its ashes ➡ 82. The Teatro La Fenice Foundation organizes the season, putting on a program worthy of a great opera house.

Teatro a l'Avogaria (2)
calle lunga San Barnaba, Dorsoduro 1607, 30123 ☎ 041 5209270

🚟 Ca' Rezzonico, San Basilio *theater* 🕐 8.30pm; public holidays 5.30pm ● *free (donations welcome)* 📠

This theater may be small (advance reservations essential), but the company, founded by Giovanni Poli, is distinguished, touring the world, with its repertoire of plays by Renaissance dramatists. Enthusiasm and professionalism certainly seem to be the driving forces here.

Teatro Fondamenta Nuove (3)
fondamente Nove, Cannaregio 5013, 30131 ☎ 041 5224498

🚟 Fondamente Nove, Ca' d'Oro *theater* 🕐 9pm; public holidays 4pm ● *10,000-16,000 lire* 📠

A futuristic atmosphere in a 16th-century warehouse, a juxtaposition of wooden beams and old marble with more modern materials. This theater has a full and varied program of plays, concerts, dance, movies, exhibitions, attracting well-known names from all branches of the arts.

Santa Maria della Pietà (4)
riva degli Schiavoni, Castello, 30122 ☎ 041 5231096

San Zaccaria **concerts** ◓ 8.30pm ● 20,000-40,000 lire ▭
@ www.vivaldi.it, www.vivaldichurch.com

In keeping with the memory of Antonio Vivaldi (the 'red priest' was choirmaster here) the Pietà holds superlative Baroque music concerts. The regular orchestra (10 players) alternates with chamber music groups.

Not forgetting

■ **Teatro Goldoni (5)** calle della Carbonera, San Marco 4650/B, 30124 ☎ 041 5205422-041 5207583 *Home to the Teatro Stabile del Veneto (the equivalent of a regional state theater company), it also plays host to French companies.* ■ **Scuola Grande di San Rocco (6)** campo San Rocco, San Polo 3052, 30125 ☎ 041 962999 ◓ 9pm Apr.-Oct. *A setting* ➡ *96, for a program of Baroque music, with a few visiting international orchestras.* ■ **San Bartolomio (7)** campo San Bartolomio, San Marco 5096, 30124 ☎ 041 2770561 ◓ 8.30pm; summer: daily; winter: Tue., Fri., Sat. *The Interpreti Veneziani specialize in period performances of Vivaldi here* ➡ *94.*

In 1683, the first *bottega del caffè* opened under the Procuratie. These coffee shops often had something of the tavern about them: low-ceilinged and windowless, they were often ill lit and sparsely furnished. A century later, there were 24 cafés in Piazza San Marco alone. Some of the original *botteghe* survive and are among the most beautiful cafés in the world.

After dark

Gran Caffè Lavena (8)
piazza San Marco, San Marco 133-134, 30124
☎ 041 5224070 ➠ 041 5200151

San Zaccaria, San Marco ⏰ *winter: 9.30am–11.30pm; summer: 9.30–12.30am; closed Tue. in winter and Jan. 7-31* 🔲 ⛔ 🎵
@ venetia@venetia.it, www.venetia.it/lavena

Richard Wagner composed some of his finest music while seated at his table at the Lavena, as a plaque inside notes. Liszt, D'Annunzio and, more recently, Alberto Moravia, were also regular customers. From its opening in 1750 until the present, this *bottega* has seen some of the most famous names in Italian and international intellectual circles come and go. The sumptuous décor, with its period furniture and Murano-glass chandeliers, ensures that the Lavena retains its romantic, very fin-de-siècle atmosphere to this day. The superb ice creams, and lemon and coffee *granitas* have also contributed to its reputation.

Gran Caffè Florian (9)
piazza San Marco, San Marco 56, 30124
☎ 041 5205641 ➠ 041 5224409

San Zaccaria, San Marco ⏰ *May-Sep.: 10-12.30am; Oct.-Apr.: 9.30am–midnight; closed Wed. in winter, one week before Christmas and one week in Jan.* 🔲 ⛔ 🎴 🎵 @ info@caffeflorian.com, www.caffeflorian.com

In 1720 an extremely elegant café opened in the long arcades below the Procuratie Nuove under the name 'Venice Triumphant', but people later called it after the first owner, Floriano Francesconi. Florian's was an immediate hit with Venetian high society. Goldoni, the Gozzi brothers and Canova enjoyed going there, as did many distinguished writers from other countries who visited Venice, among them Goethe, Rousseau and Balzac who described Florian's as a stock exchange, theater foyer, reading room, a club, and a confessional, all rolled into one. The six small rooms (known as the Room of Famous Men, the Four Seasons Room, the Oriental Room, the Chinese Room, the Senate Room and the Liberty Room) have valuable, 18th-century furniture and fittings in which gilt and purple velvet upholstery predominate. From April until the end of October, an orchestra (the 'Caffè Concerto') helps to keep Venice's musical traditions alive.

Gran Caffè Quadri (10)
piazza San Marco, San Marco 121, 30124
☎ 041 5222105 ➠ 041 5208041

San Zaccaria, San Marco ⏰ *summer: 9–12.30am; winter: 9am–11.30pm; closed Mon. in winter* 🔲 ⛔ 🎵 @ caffequadri@libero.it

Seated at little tables, cosseted by attentive waiters and surrounded by gilded mirrors and stuccos of floral motifs, Quadri's customers can almost imagine themselves in the state apartments of a royal palace. Opened in 1775, this is another café that has welcomed a succession of celebrities visiting La Serenissima: Byron, Ruskin, Dumas, Proust and Wagner (when he was being unfaithful to the Lavena). Pause for a leisurely drink on the terrace, not least because the view of St Mark's Basilica, the Doge's Palace and the Procuratie Nuove from here is particularly captivating. An orchestra provides music from April to October.

8

Venetian history has been influenced by the habitués of these cafés in Piazza San Marco, each a unique stage set, in a vast theater.

9

10

10

Although the *campi* have a somewhat Mediterranean feel to them, ideal for a desultory chat, perched on a bench or on the edge of a well, Venice's cafés are typical of a northern Italian city: at the first hint of winter, the inhabitants head for a snug corner in one of the traditional *bacari* where they can set the world to rights over a couple of *ombre* and a few *cicheti*.

After dark

La Colombina (11)
sottoportico del Pegolotto, Cannaregio 1828, 30121
☎ 041 2750622 ➠ 041 2750622

San Marcuola **bacaro-wine bar** *noon–3pm, 6pm–2am; closed Sun. and lunchtime Mon.*

Small, welcoming and comfortable, La Colombina opened less than a year ago but has proved an immediate success: people come here to sip an *ombra* (preferably white wine), to peruse the latest newspapers, or for a quick snack. There is a huge choice of wines: around a dozen are sold by the carafe and over a hundred are on the wine list. In the kitchen, great store is set by serving freshly caught fish, prepared with flair. In summer, tables are set up outside, on the *campiello*, and diners are serenaded by groups or orchestras that turn up to enliven the evening with popular or classical music.

All'Arco (12)
ruga Vecchia San Giovanni, San Polo 436
30125 ☎ 041 5205666

San Silvestro, Rialto, San Stae **bacaro** *8am–4pm, 6.30–10pm, Sat. 8am–4pm; closed Sun.*

This *bacaro* of many years' standing has recently become the haunt of Venetian 'thirty-somethings' who like to meet here and sit around a table under the stars. A wide variety of wines are sold by the carafe for *ombre*, and traditional *cicheti*, are available; among the latter the more adventurous may want to sample *tetina* and *rumegal*.

Vino Vino (13)
ponte delle Veste, San Marco 2007/A, 30124
☎ 041 2417688 ➠ 041 5289857

San Marco, Santa Maria del Giglio **wine bar-osteria** *10.30am–midnight; closed Tue.* @ vinovino@anticomartini.com

Situated in one of the busiest parts of the city, this outstanding wine bar also serves delicious simple meals. There is a wide choice of bottled wines (about 350 good Italian and foreign varieties to drink here or take out) and the house wines sold by the carafe are excellent. A predominantly Venetian clientele, well aware of the favorable price:quality equation, but a growing number of tourists are getting to hear about it. For a quick meal, there are several traditional dishes (listed on a board by the entrance) or a fixed menu. Orders taken at the bar.

Cantina Do Mori (14)
calle dei Due Mori, San Polo 429, 30125 ☎ 041 5225401

San Silvestro, Rialto, San Stae **wine bar-bacaro** *8.30am-8.30pm; closed Sun.*

One of the oldest *osterie* in Venice, and among the most famous in the Rialto district. Visitors cannot fail to be charmed by the place, with its copper pans hanging from the ceiling. The likeable and convivial owners are well qualified to offer advice on what to choose from the extensive cellar (200 bottled wines and 130 wines sold by the glass) to accompany their unusual *cicheti*. There is just one drawback: Do Mori closes far too early!

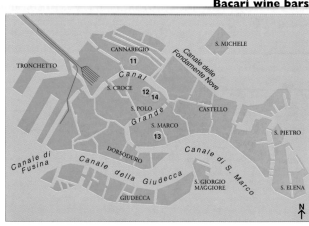

11

12

13

12

14

To the dismay of their parents and grandparents, young Venetians are deserting the traditional *bacari* for more 'international' drinking places where the beer flows freely. Venice has had to adapt to this change in fashion and a sprinkling of pubs and beer bars are now doing good business, staying open until the early hours.

After dark

Piero e Mauro (15)
calle dei Fabbri, San Marco 881, 30124 ☎ 041 5237756

San Zaccaria, San Marco **bar** ⏰ 6.30am–2am

Just behind Piazza San Marco; a tiny bar popular with young Venetians and foreigners. The glasses are suspended over the bar, the bottles form part of the décor, the tables are small… but the banquettes are comfortable. Customers can order *crostini, panini* and *tramezzini* (sandwiches made with rye bread), beers and several varieties of *grappa* (a Venetian type of brandy). A cool place to be in the early hours of the morning.

Bacaro Jazz (16)
**salizzada San Giovanni Crisostomo, Cannaregio 5546
30124 ☎ 041 285249**

Rialto **bacaro-wine bar** ⏰ 11am–2am; closed Wed. ▭ @ bacarojazz@iol.it

The name reflects the owner's love of jazz. This *bacaro* now has a young and modern feel, halfway between a beer bar and a traditional *osteria*. There is not only a wide range of beers and cocktails, but also *cicheti* and wine, sold by the glass. The kitchen produces pizzas and traditional Italian dishes. Subdued lighting with jazz for background music.

The Fiddler's Elbow (17)
**corte dei Pali, Cannaregio 3847, 30131
☎ 041 5239930 ➠ 041 5239930**

Ca' d'Oro **Irish pub** ⏰ 5pm–12.30am

A pub straight out of the 'island of saints and giants' frequented by a clientele of young Venetians, students and foreign tourists who come here for a get-together over a good draft beer. A chance to become further acquainted with *stouts*, those dark brown, hoppy beers, with highly roasted barley added to their brewing malts, Cashel's cider, and the more famous Irish coffee. The only place of its kind in Venice showing British satellite television channels.

Caffè Noir (18)
**calle San Pantalon, Dorsoduro 3805, 30123
☎ 041 710925 ➠ 041 2756300**

San Tomà **cyber café** ⏰ Mon.-Sat. 7–2am; Sun. 9–2am ● 10,000 lire per 1hr online time ▭ 🕮 🍴 🔲 📷 @ cafenoir@flashnet.it

Internet freaks have their own room where they can surf to their heart's content; others will enjoy the chance to compare notes in the larger, main room with its friendly atmosphere and soft lighting. Light toasted snacks, croissants and sandwiches; beer, *grappas* (brandies), hot chocolate and a variety of teas.

Not forgetting

■ **L'Olandese Volante (19)** campo San Lio, Castello 5658, 30122 ☎ 041 5289349 ⏰ 11–1am *50 varieties of beer – of which five are draft beers sold 'by the meter': in boxes one meter (3 ft) long, each containing eight tankards.*
■ **Margaret DuChamp (20)** campo San Margherita, Dorsoduro 3019, 30123 ☎ 041 5286255 ⏰ 9am-2am, Sat. noon-2am. *Where students meet.*

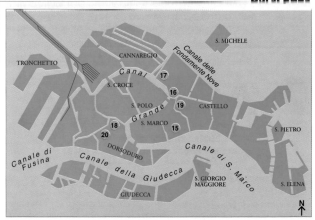

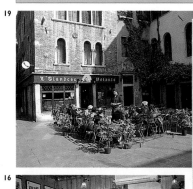

Devotees of both traditional and
modern jazz are agreed that Bacaro
Jazz caters for all tastes.

➡ **What to see**

Piazza San Marco

Thanks to an agreement between the Ministry of Culture and the city authorities, it is possible to visit the monuments of 'the world's drawing room' without spending a fortune: the special **Itinerario Marciano** ticket gives access to the Doges' Palace, the Libreria Sansoviniana (archeological museum and St Mark's library), the Correr Museum and all of Venice's municipal museums. For information: **APT/IAT** *Castello 4421, 30122* ☎ *0415298711* ➡ *0415230399* ➡ *15*

Churches

The churches of Venice house many great masterpieces. Thanks to the Chorus association, it is now possible to visit these places of worship at all times of day by purchasing a single admission ticket. The proceeds go toward restoring what is the city's greatest 'museum'.

Chorus ☎ *041 2750462* ➡ *041 2750494* @ *chorus@tin.it, www.chorus-ve.org*

107
Sights

Venice was founded in the 6th century, when the inhabitants of the Roman province of Venetia fled to the Adriatic coast and islands to escape the invading Lombards. The city state's galleys were soon plying the Adriatic and the entire Mediterranean, bringing home the colors, fragrances and precious merchandise of the Orient.

What to see

(7) ➥ 78

(11) ➥ 80

(22) ➥ 84

(30) ➥ 88

(36) ➥ 90

Basilica di San Marco ➥ 78
St. Mark's Basilica is named after Venice's patron saint, whose relics were brought there from Constantinople in 829. It is nicknamed the 'golden church' because of the 43,000 sq ft of mosaics (12th–14th centuries).

The Doges' Palace ➥ 80
Residence of the Doges and seat of government, this flamboyant Gothic masterpiece was decorated by the greatest artists of the 16th-century Venetian school.

Ca' Rezzonico ➥ 84
This palace, with rooms decorated by Tiepolo, houses a museum devoted to 18th-century decorative art.

Galleria dell' Accademia ➥ 88
The Venetian school in all its splendor, featuring works from Bellini to Canaletto.

Santa Maria della Salute ➥ 90
The most harmonious example of Baroque architecture, designed by Longhena.

Santa Maria Gloriosa dei Frari ➥ 96
This pantheon of the Republic's great men is the city's largest church and one of the most commodious ever erected by a religious order. It houses works by Titian, Giovanni Bellini and Donatello.

Ghetto ➥ 102
From 1516 to 1797, the Jews were confined to this district, the only entrance to which was closed at night-time.

Madonna dell'Orto ➥ 104
More than any other, this church is associated with Tintoretto. He painted a number of masterpieces for it while still a young man, and is buried there.

Santa Maria dei Miracoli ➥ 108
A Renaissance jewel, the interior is entirely clad in marquetry and polychrome marble.

SS. Giovanni e Paolo ➥ 110
A grandiose expression of Gothic art, the tombs of 25 of the Republic's Doges are in this church.

(53) ➥ 96

(71) ➥ 102

(74) ➥ 104

(87) ➥ 108

(89) ➥ 110

S. MICHELE

**MADONNA
DELL'ORTO**
★

GHETTO
★

CANAREGIO

Canale delle Fondamente Nove

Canal

Grande

S. CROCE

**SS. GIOVANNI
E PAOLO**
★

**S. MARIA
DEI MIRACOLI**
★

CASTELLO

S. POLO

Grande

**S. MARIA G.
DEI FRARI**
★

Canal

S. MARCO

S.MARCO
★

PAL. DUCALE
★

**CA'
EZZONICO**
★

Bacino di S. Marco

**GALLERIE
DELL'ACCADEMIA**
★

**S. MARIA
DELLA SALUTE**
★

DORSODURO

S. GIORGIO
MAGGIORE

Giudecca

Canale   della

GIUDECCA

N
↑

The importance and variety of Venetian festivals and parades turn the city into a theatrical stage. There are such crowds at these events that rules have to be laid down for pedestrian traffic! This is, however, when it is most obvious that Venice knows how to extend a warm welcome to those 'foreigners' who have come to explore her.

What to see

Carnevale (1)

End Jan. – Shrove Tue. @ *www.carnivalvenice.it*

Officially, *Carnevale* starts on Maundy Thursday but preparations last for months. After lapsing for a century, the custom of celebrating *Carnevale* was revived in 1980 and this is by far the most popular Venetian festival. The main venue is still Piazza San Marco but all the *campi* and *campielli* are invaded by joyful crowds, some in most unusual disguises, rubbing shoulders with others who prefer traditional costumes – the *bauta* (a black silk hood and a lace cape) and the *tabarrot*: a large black cape, a tricorne hat and white mask. A succession of balls, theatrical performances and cultural events culminates in the burning of the carnival effigy in Piazza San Marco.

Festa della Sensa (2)

Second Sun. in May @ *www.comune.venezia.it, www.provincia.venezia.it/aptve*

The ceremony of the Marriage of Venice and the Sea used to take place on Ascension Day. The Doge sailed out into the open sea in his galley and threw a ring into the sea, his 'wife'; in this way Venice affirmed her domination of the Adriatic. The Mayor of Venice keeps up the tradition, a pretext for a great maritime festival in which hundreds of vessels take part.

Festa del Redentore (3)

Third Sun. in July @ *www.comune.venezia.it, www.provincia.venezia.it/aptve*

In 1576, during an epidemic of plague, Doge Alvise Mocenigo vowed to build a church on the island of Giudecca. In 1578, barges formed a bridge, linking the two shores of St Mark's basin, enabling crowds of Venetians to make their way to the tabernacle on the site of the future church, in order to praise God for having spared them. Nowadays the bridge of barges is put in place on the eve of this festival and the climax comes at midnight, with a firework display.

Regata storica (4)

First Sun. in Sep. @ *www.comune.venezia.it, www.provincia.venezia.it/aptve*

The present-day regatta commemorates that held on January 10, 1315 when for the first time symbolic prizes of colored banners (a red one for the overall winner) were presented to the victors. Before the race, in which traditional lagoon craft compete in four separate contests, a historical procession takes place: behind the *Bucentaur* come the *bissone*, large barges with eight oars, then the gondolas, all carrying crowds of people in fancy dress.

Festa della Salute (5)

Nov. 21 @ *www.comune.venezia.it, www.provincia.venezia.it/aptve*

This festival also originated with a vow made by the Doge and Senate during another great epidemic of plague, in 1630: this vow led to the construction of the church of Santa Maria della Salute. Nowadays the Patriarch of Venice leads the procession of the faithful over the bridge of barges placed across the Grand Canal. After lighting a candle on the altar dedicated to the Virgin Mary, Venetians crowd around stalls set up near the church, selling cookies baked for this occasion.

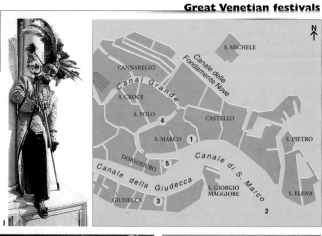

In the area
- ➡ **Where to stay:** ➡ 20
- ➡ **Where to eat:** ➡ 40 ➡ 54
- ➡ **After dark:** ➡ 64 ➡ 68
- ➡ **Where to shop:** ➡ 132

What to see

Piazza San Marco (6)

San Marco

At the top of the *Campanile*, built at the end of the 15th century, two bronze statues – the 'moors' – strike the hours in Piazza San Marco, 'Europe's finest drawing-room'. St Mark's Basilica, once the Doges' chapel, forms the backdrop for this theatrical setting, framed by the long, arcaded buildings of the Procuratie, formerly the offices of the Procurators of St Mark, the most senior magistrates in the Republic after the Doge: to the north the Procuratie Vecchie (12th–16th century); to the south, the Procuratie nuove, begun in 1586 by Scamozzi and completed by Longhena in 1640. Beneath the Procuratie are numerous shops and cafés; the most famous – Florian's and Quadri's – dating from the 18th century ➡ 64.

Basilica di San Marco (7)
piazza San Marco, 30124 ☎ 041 5225697

San Marco ◷ 9.45am–5.30pm ● free *Pala d'Oro* ◷ 9.45am–5.30pm ● 1,500-3,000 lire *Treasury* ◷ 9.45am–5.30pm, Sun. and public holidays 1.30–5.30pm ● > 2,000 lire (group tour) – 4,000 lire *Museum di San Marco* ◷ 9.45am–5.30pm ● 1,500–3,000 lire

In his *Translation of the Body of St Mark*, now in the Gallerie dell'Accademia, Tintoretto illustrates the legend of Rustico and Buono, merchants from Torcello, who discovered the Apostle's remains in Alexandria and brought these back with them to Venice in 828. This led to the building of a church to house the saint's bones. Consecrated in 1094, the basilica was the third place of worship erected on this site; the central plan, in the shape of a Greek cross, and the series of cupolas are clear evidence of Byzantine influence. From the 11th to the 15th century, successive changes resulted in the basilica as we now know it. The gilded bronze horses on the upper terrace were plunder from the Crusaders' sack of Byzantium, during the Fourth Crusade (1204); Doge Enrico Dandolo had them brought back to Venice (they have since been replaced by copies and the originals are now exhibited in St Mark's Museum). The interior decoration – the mosaics on the walls, the floor of marble with its 12th-century mosaics and the Pala d'Oro, an incomparable masterpiece of the goldsmith's art – made San Marco a 'golden church', its richness mirroring that of the Serene Republic.

Museo Correr (8)
piazza San Marco 52, 30124 ☎ 041 5225625

San Marco ◷ Apr.–Oct. 9am-7pm; Nov.–Mar. 9 am–5pm ● 10,000–18,000 lire; ticket also valid for municipal museums, Doge's Palace, Libreria Sansoviniana

Apart from the rooms devoted to the history of Venice, recording the past glories of the Republic, the visitor can admire a fine group by the sculptor Antonio Canova (1757–1822), considered the most outstanding member of the neoclassical school. ★ The art gallery houses many masterpieces: *Two Venetian Ladies* by Carpaccio (c. 1465–c. 1525), a *Pietà* (1475–1476) by Antonello da Messina and another by Cosmé Tura of Ferrara (c. 1468); the Bellini room contains works by Jacopo, Gentile and Giovanni Bellini, a family of painters active from the 15th century until 1516; the Alvise Vivarini room contains works by this painter who also belonged to a family of artists from Murano (15th–early 16th century).

In the area
- ▪️ **Where to stay:** ➡ 18 ➡ 34
- ▪️ **Where to eat:** ➡ 40 ➡ 42
- ▪️ **After dark:** ➡ 63 ➡ 64
- ▪️ **Where to shop:** ➡ 132

What to see

Piazzetta San Marco (9)

▦ San Marco

The two columns of Egyptian granite, one surmounted by the warrior saint, St Theodore, the city's former patron saint, supplanted by St Mark; the other by a lion symbolizing the apostle, used to mark the official gateway into Venice which could only be entered from the sea. The square is bordered by the façade of the Doges' Palace, the *Campanile* and the 16th-century Libreria Marciana, built by Jacopo Sansovino.

Campanile di San Marco (10)
piazza San Marco, 30124 ☎ 041 5225205

▦ San Marco 🕐 *summer: 9am–9.30pm; winter: 9.30am–5.30pm* ● *4,000–8,000 lire* ▦

Originally a simple watchtower, it was changed and its height increased several times during the course of 12th, 14th and 16th centuries. It collapsed on July 14, 1902 and was rebuilt 'as and how it used to be', in 1912. At its foot, the Loggetta de Sansovino (1537-1549, completed in the 17th century with a terrace and a balustrade) was also faithfully restored.

Palazzo Ducale (11)
piazzetta San Marco, 30124 ☎ 041 5224951

▦ San Marco 🕐 *Apr.–Oct.: 9am–5.30pm; Nov–Mar. 9am–3.30pm* ● *10,000–18,000 lire; ticket also valid for Museo Correr, municipal museums, Libreria Sansovina* 🎫 *by arrangement* ▦ ▢ ♿

The earlier building on this site resembled a fortified castle: defended by high walls, with two corner towers. From the 14th to the16th centuries it underwent many changes, resulting in its present appearance. The two wings, rebuilt in 1340 and 1424, look out over St Mark's basin and onto the Piazzetta, a fine example of Gothic architecture, with its galleries and arcades supporting the structure of the upper story, decorated with sober, geometric patterns. Through the Porta della Carta, a masterpiece by the Venetian 'stone-cutters' (masons) Giovanni and Bartolomeo Bon, the visitor gains entrance to the interior courtyard. An arch gives directly onto the Giants' Stairway (late 15th century, Antonio Rizzo), at the top of which are statues of Neptune and Mars. ★ The great council chamber contains Tintoretto's *Paradise* and several works by Veronese, Leandro Bassano and Palma Giovane. The palace was both the Doge's residence and the headquarters of government. It was also a prison: the *Pozzi* (wells) on the ground floor and the *Piombi* (leads) under the roof achieved worldwide notoriety after Casanova claimed to have escaped from them.

Not forgetting

▪️ **Libreria Sansoviniana (12)** piazzetta San Marco 13, 30124 ☎ 041 5225978 🕐 *Apr.–Oct.: 9am–7pm; Nov.–Mar.: 9am–5pm* ● *10,000–18,000 lire, ticket also valid for Palazzo Ducale, municipal museums, Museo Correr Home to the library and the Archeological Museum.*

▪️ **Ponte dei Sospiri (13)** ponte della Paglia *Built at the very end of the 16th century, the Bridge of Sighs links the Doge's Palace with the New Prisons. It acquired its name in the 19th century, prompted by the sighs (sospiri) of condemned prisoners as they crossed it on their way to prison.*

Piazza S. Marco   10
PROCURATIE NUOVE   MUSEO
ARCHEOLOGICO
Rio della Zecca   12   Piazzetta   13
S. Marco   11
GIARDINI EX REALI   9
Fondam. d. Farine   Molo

Lacework of carved stone on the façade facing St Mark's basin, with a balcony by Dalle Masegne (1404).

In the area

 Where to stay: ➡ 22
 Where to eat: ➡ 40 ➡ 42
 After dark: ➡ 66
 Where to shop: ➡ 132 ➡ 134 ➡ 136

➡ What to see

San Moisè (14)
campo San Moisè, San Marco, 30124 ☎ 041 5285840

San Marco 3.30–7pm; Sun. 9am–noon, 3.30–7pm ● free

The existing building is the fourth church on this site. It dates from 1668 and is by Alessandro Tremignon, commissioned by two Venetians, Vincenzo and Gerolamo Fini, whose effigies appear on the façade. The high altar, also designed by Tremignon and executed by the sculptor, Meyling, a disciple of Bernini; *The Washing of the Feet* by Tintoretto and a *Last Supper* attributed to Palma Giovane, are all worthy of note.

Teatro La Fenice (15)
campo San Fantin, San Marco, 30124

Santa Maria del Giglio **Palafenice** ➡ 62

The famous theater is one of the Europe's most illustrious opera houses; first performances of works by Rossini, Donizetti and Verdi took place here; in 1951 La Fenice staged the première of Stravinsky's *The Career of a Libertine* and, more recently, of compositions by Verio, Nono and Bussotti. It opened in 1792 with an opera by Giovanni Paisiello, *The Games of Agrigento*. The name – the phoenix was a bird that was reborn from its ashes – was meant to reflect a fiery past: its predecessor, the San Benedetto opera house, had been destroyed by fire in 1774. Fire continued to take its toll: the first Fenice went up in flames during the night of May 12–13, 1836; the restoration was entrusted to Meduna and the new, redecorated, theater auditorium opened the following year, on the evening of December 26. On January 29, 1996 the opera house was again destroyed by fire; this time, bureaucratic red tape has considerably delayed reconstruction, but the opening night's program has already been announced: it is to be one of Wagner's operas, staged by Bob Wilson. This is scheduled for 2001.

Santa Maria del Giglio (16)
campo Santa Maria del Giglio, San Marco, 30124 ☎ 041 2750462

Santa Maria del Giglio 10am–5pm, Sun. 1–5pm ● 3,000 lire (group tour)

This church is also called Santa Maria Zobenigo, from the name of a very old Slav family whose palace used to stand nearby and who are thought to have contributed to the cost of the original edifice. ★ *Virgin and Child with St John*, attributed to Rubens, Tintoretto's *Apostles* and portraits by Palma Giovane.

Not forgetting

■ **Palazzo Contarini del Bovolo (17)** corte del Bovolo, San Marco 4299, 30124 ☎ 041 2702464 Apr.–Oct.: 10am–6pm ● 2,000–3,000 lire. *This palace was built for the Contarini family during the 15th and 16th centuries. The loggias on the façade are linked by a round tower containing a spiral staircase from which the palace takes its full, descriptive name: the Contarini Palace del Bovolo 'of the snail', and its airy beauty has no equal.* ■ **Campo Sant'Angelo (18)** *Always bustling, named after a church dedicated to the Archangel Michael which was demolished in 1837. Numerous palaces of great Venetian families surround this campo. The oratory of the Santissima Annunziata contains an* Annunciation *by Palma Giovane.*

The façade of San Moisè, covered with exuberant decoration, is typically Baroque.

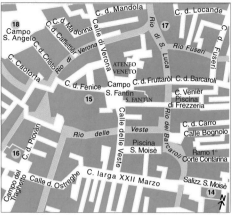

➡ **Where to stay:** ➡ 22 ➡ 24
➡ **Where to eat:** ➡ 42 ➡ 48
➡ **After dark:** ➡ 66
➡ **Where to shop:** ➡ 134 ➡ 138

What to see

Campo Santo Stefano (19)

▦ *Accademia*

This square has to be crossed when walking from the Accademia to San Marco or the Rialto and has always been a place to meet, where people go to 'see and be seen'. In the center stands the statue of the patriot and literary figure Niccolo Tommaseo (1802–74).

Santo Stefano (20)
campo Santo Stefano, San Marco, 30124 ☎ 041 2750462

▦ *Accademia* 🕐 *10am–5pm, Sun. 1–5pm* ● *3,000 lire (group tour)*

Commissioned in the late 13th century by the Augustine Order, this Gothic church underwent considerable alteration during the first half of the 15th century. ★ The interior, with its ship's keel ceiling, retains the choir stalls of the Augustine friars, paintings by Bartolomeo Vivarìni, Palma Vecchio, Marieschi and Tintorettò, and funerary monuments.

Palazzo Grassi (21)
campo San Samuele, San Marco, 30124 ☎ 041 5231680

▦ *San Samuele* 🕐 *exhibitions 10am–7pm* ● *varies* 🏧 🍴 *Cipriani* 📷 ♿

This palace was built for the Grassi family, gentry from Chioggia who were admitted into the Venetian aristocracy in return for payment of 60,000 ducats in 1718 to help finance the war against the Turks. The Grassi commissioned Massari to supervise the building of this palace, one of the most important examples of 18th-century civil architecture, and the last great palace built before the fall of the Serenissima. In 1984 it was purchased by Fiat which entrusted the restoration to Gae Aulenti and Antonio Foscari, since when it has been used for major artistic exhibitions.

Ca' Rezzonico (22)
calle di Ca' Rezzonico, Dorsoduro 3136, 30123

▦ *Ca' Rezzonico* ☎ *041 2418506–2410100* 🕐 *Museum of 18th-century Venice undergoing restoration*

Only the ground floor and first floor, built for the Bon family by Longhena from 1667 onward, were complete when the architect died in 1682. After the family's downfall, it remained unfinished until it was acquired by the Rezzonico family in 1751. Massari was commissioned to complete the work: he built the second floor and had a hand in designing the interior, most notably the largest ballroom in Venice. In 1934 the palace was purchased by the city and turned into a museum of 18th-century Venice: paintings, furniture and faïence, as well as collections from various Venetian residences, are exhibited in rooms decorated by Tiepolo.

Not forgetting

■ **Campo San Maurizio (23)** *Named after its church rebuilt in 1806, this square is also home to the Scuola degli Albanesi, its façade (1531) decorated with Renaissance bas-reliefs. Around Christmas an antiques market is held here.*
■ **Ca' Foscari (24)** *calle di Ca' Foscari, Dorsoduro 3246, 30123 ☎ 041 5206122* 🕐 *undergoing restoration. Built for Doge Francesco Foscari, this palace was for many years occupied by the University.*

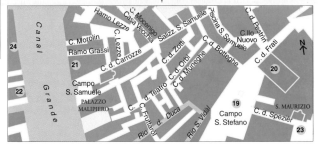

Ca' Foscari, 'wrapped' to hide restoration work: a huge *trompe-l'oeil* painting of the façade prevents any break in the continuous spectacle of palaces lining the Grand Canal.

In the area
- **Where to stay:** ➡ 28
- **Where to eat:** ➡ 48
- **After dark:** ➡ 62 ➡ 70
- **Where to shop:** ➡ 142

What to see

San Sebastiano (25)
salizzada San Basegio, Dorsoduro, 30123 ☎ 041 2750462

San Basilio ⏰ 10am–5pm, Sun. 3–5pm ● 3,000 lire (group tour)

Built at the end of 17th century by Scarpagnino: this church provides a simple setting for one of the finest cycles ever painted by Veronese. He began with the *Coronation of the Virgin* (1555) which adorns the sacristy ceiling, followed by three large paintings of scenes from the life of Esther (1556), on the ceiling of the nave, and then by *The Annunciation*; figures of a Sybil and of saints (1558) and, finally, by the great paintings in the main chapel (1565). Veronese was buried in this church as he wished.

Palazzo Zenobio (26)
fondamenta del Soccorso, Dorsoduro 2596, 30123

San Basilio, Ca' Rezzonico **Armenian College** ☎ 041 5228770
⏰ by arrangement ● free

Built at the end of the 17th century by Antonio Gaspari, who was a pupil of Longhena, this is one of the finest examples of Baroque civil architecture in Venice. The interior is typical of 18th-century Venetian interior decoration: the *vedutas* of the *portego* were executed by one of Venice's foremost view painters, Luca Carlevaris; in the ballroom, with its white and gold stuccos, the architectural perspectives painted in trompe-l'oeil make the room seem even more enormous than it is.

Santa Maria del Carmelo o Carmini (27)
campo dei Carmini, Dorsoduro, 30123 ☎ 041 5226553

San Basilio, Ca' Rezzonico ⏰ 7.30am–noon, 3–7pm, Sun. 4.30–7.30pm ● free

The original construction dates back to the end of the 13th century but at the beginning of the 16th century a Renaissance-style façade was added by Sebastiano da Lugano and, in the mid-17th century, the interior of the nave was covered in carved and gilded wood.★ Most worthy of note: a *Nativity* by Cima da Conegliano (c. 1509), a reredos by Lotto depicting *The Apotheosis of St Nicholas* (c. 1529) and a bas relief in bronze, *The Deposition*, attributed to Francesco Giorgio Martini.

Scuola Grande dei Carmini (28)
campo dei Carmini, Dorsoduro, 30123 ☎ 041 5289420

San Basilio, Ca' Rezzonico ⏰ Apr.–Oct. 9am–6pm, Sun. 9am–1pm; Nov.–Mar.: 9am–4pm; Sun. 9am–1pm ● 6,000–8,000 lire

Originally only women could join the Order of Notre-Dame-du-Mont-Carmel. At the end of the 16th century men were admitted and, during the latter 17th century they entrusted Longhena with the construction of their *scuola*. ★ The upper room was decorated by Giambattista Tiepolo between 1739 and 1749: in the center of the ceiling is *The Apparition of Notre-Dame-du-Mont-Carmel to the Blessed Simeon Stock*.

Not forgetting

■ **Angelo Raffaele (29)** campo Angelo Raffaele, Dorsoduro, 30123 ☎ 041 522848 ⏰ 8.30am–noon, 4–6pm ● free *Beautifully decorated organ parapet, with five panels by Gianantonio Guardi, brother of Francesco.*

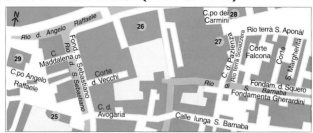

In the area

▶ **Where to stay:** ➡ 28
▶ **Where to eat:** ➡ 48
▶ **After dark:** ➡ 62 ➡ 68
▶ **Where to shop:** ➡ 142

➡

What to see

Gallerie dell'Accademia (30)
campo della Carità, Dorsoduro 1080, 30123 ☎ 041 5222247

▦ *Accademia* 🕐 *Mon. 9am–2pm, Tue.–Fri. 9am–9pm, Sat. 9am–11pm, Sun. 9am–8pm* ● *12,000 lire* ▦ ▣ ♿

The Academy of Fine Arts was founded by the Senate in 1750. In 1807, ten years after the fall of the Republic, the art gallery was opened to provide a study resource for the Accademia's pupils and also to house Venice's artistic inheritance which had been widely dispersed by this time as a result of the Serenissima's misfortunes. The Accademia was established in the former Carità church and in the premises of the Scuola Santa Maria della Carità. ★ Here the visitor is provided with an exceptional panorama of Venetian painting, from the 14th to the 18th century, including the major works of the greatest artists who were active in Venice: Paolo and Lorenzo Veneziano (14th century); Giovanni Bellini; Carpaccio (15th century); Giorgione; Titian, Tintoretto, Veronese, Lorenzo Lotto (16th century); Tiepolo, Piazzetta, Longhi, Rosalba Carriera (17th–18th centuries).

San Trovaso (31)
campo San Trovaso, Dorsoduro, 30123 ☎ 041 5222133

▦ *Zattere* 🕐 *8–11am, 3–6pm, closed Sun.* ● *free*

The name derives from a contraction of the names of two martyred saints to whom the church is dedicated, Gervasio and Protasio. Founded in the 9th or 10th century, the church was altered several times before it was rebuilt at the end of the 16th century in Palladian style, with two identical facades, one facing the square, the other on the *rio*. Inside are paintings by Tintoretto, Palma Giovane and a superlative Renaissance bas-relief.

I Gesuati (32)
fondamenta Zattere ai Gesuati, Dorsoduro, 30123 ☎ 041 5230625

▦ *Zattere* 🕐 *9am–6pm, Sun. 1–6pm* ● *3,000 lire*

This church takes its name from the former owners of the site, the Jesuates, an order whose mission was to care for the sick and which was suppressed in 1668. Their premises and lands were handed over to the Dominicans who, in 1724, asked Massari to build a new church, completed in 1736. The interior is one of the most beautiful examples of Rococo decorative schemes to be found anywhere in Venice.

Fondamenta delle Zattere (33)

▦ *Zattere* 🍴

In a bygone era this quay was where all the wood that was shipped to Venice had to be landed, whence its name 'zattere' (timber raft). Nowadays this is the place to find some of the best ice cream in the whole city: the *gianduiotto* is particularly delicious!

Not forgetting

■ **Squero di San Trovaso (34)** campo San Trovaso, Dorsoduro, 30123 *Gondola yard dating from the 17th century.*

31
34

The San Trovaso *squero* is one of the last working gondola yards in Venice; once there were hundreds of these workshops, busily building and repairing gondolas.

30

In the area
- **➡ Where to stay:** ➡ 22 ➡ 28
- **➡ Where to eat:** ➡ 48
- **➡ After dark:** ➡ 64 ➡ 68
- **➡ Where to shop:** ➡ 134

What to see

Collezione Peggy Guggenheim (35)
calle San Gregorio, Dorsoduro 701, 30123 ☎ 041 5206288

▦ *Accademia, Salute* ◷ *11am–6pm; closed Tue.* ● *8,000–12,000 lire* ▦ *by appoinment* ▦ ▦ ▦

In 1949 Peggy Guggenheim (1898–1979) bought the Venier dei Leoni palace, whose construction had been commenced in 1749, but was never totally finished. Since 1976, the museum has been administered by the Solomon R. Guggenheim Foundation. The palace houses one of the world's most important modern art collections, in which all the main avant-garde artists of the first half of the 20th century are represented.

Santa Maria della Salute (36)
campo della Salute, Dorsoduro, 30123 ☎ 041 5225558

▦ *Salute* ◷ *9am–5.30pm* ● *free*

In October 1630, as a thanksgiving to the Virgin Mary for the end of a terrible epidemic of plague, the Senate commissioned Baldassare Longhena (1598-1682) to build this votive church. The building was completed by Antonio Gaspari, constructed in white Istrian stone, surmounted by two domes and flanked by two bell towers. Inside, the high altar was also designed by Longhena; the statues are the work of Josse le Court (1670), and there are fine paintings by Luca Giordano, Titian, Tintoretto and Palma Giovane. Every year the Festa della Salute commemorates the mercy shown to the city by the Virgin Mary ➡ 76.

Punta della Dogana (37)

▦ *Salute* ▦

The name comes from the Dogana da mar: the headquarters of the Venetian maritime customs service was established here in the 15th century. Between 1677 and 1682, their premises were rebuilt by the architect Giuseppe Benoni who arranged the warehouses in groups of parallel buildings behind a single façade. He replaced the crenellated tower with a low building, enhanced by a portico and a small white tower surmounted by a golden globe, on which is enthroned the goddess Fortuna, attributed to Bernardo Falcone. ★ In 2001, the Guggenheim Museum of New York is to move some of its collections into these buildings, restored by Vittorio Gregotti, where they will be exhibited with works by Italian artists (Vedova, Clemente, Cucchi).

Not forgetting

■ **Collezione Vittorio Cini (38)** campo San Vio, Dorsoduro 864, 30123 ☎ 041 5210755 ◷ 10am–1pm, 2–6pm; closed Mon. and Sep.–Dec. ● *8,000 lire Count Vittorio Cini (who died in 1977) put his impressive collection of applied arts and paintings of the Ferrara and Tuscan schools (13th–15th centuries) on display in his family's Renaissance palace.* ■ **Seminario Patriarcale (39)** campo della Salute, Dorsoduro, 30123 ☎ 041 5225558 ◷ *by arrangement Rebuilt by Longhena while he was also engaged upon the construction of Santa Maria della Salute, this building now houses the Manfrediniana art gallery and its collection of 15th–18th-century paintings and statues, bequeathed by Marchese Federico Manfredini (1743–1829).*

In the area

➔ **Where to stay:** ➡ 19 ➡ 28
➔ **Where to eat:** ➡ 42 ➡ 48
➔ **After dark:** ➡ 62 ➡ 64
➔ **Where to shop:** ➡ 134 ➡ 142

➔ What to see

Sant'Eufemia (40)
fondamenta rio di Sant'Eufemia, Giudecca, 30133 ☎ 041 5225848

▥ *Sant'Eufemia* 🕑 *9–11am, Sun. 7–11.30am* ● *free*

Founded in the 9th century, the church has retained its nave and side-aisles from the original basilica as well as some Veneto-Byzantine capitals from the 11th-century reconstruction. During the mid-18th-century restoration, the interior was decorated with frescos (1764) by the 19-year-old Canaletto, inspired by Tiepolo's achievements in the Jesuate church ➡ 88.

Il Redentore (41)
campo del Redentore, Giudecca, 30133 ☎ 041 5231415

▥ *Redentore* 🕑 *8am–noon, 4–6.30pm* ● *free*

As with Santa Maria della Salute ➡ 90, this is a votive church, the Senate having decided upon its construction in 1576, during a plague epidemic. Building got under way in 1577 under the direction of Palladio; when he died in 1580, Antonio da Ponte took over and saw the project through to its completion in 1592. ★ In the interior of the church, the reredos was commissioned from the best artists of the day. Each year, in July, the Feast of the Redeemer commemorates the Senate's vow ➡ 76.

San Giorgio Maggiore (42)
isola di San Giorgio Maggiore, 30124 ☎ 041 5227827

▥ *San Giorgio* 🕑 *10am–12.30pm, 2.30–6.30pm, Sun. 9.30–10.30am, 2.30–6pm* ● *free*

This church was designed by Andrea Palladio in 1566, but completed by Simeone Sorella around 1590. The façade, in white Istrian stone, repeats features of ancient Greek temples: the triangular pediment and the pronaos (portico) with four columns. ★ On the high altar there is a bronze group (1591–3) by Campagna; paintings by Tintoretto, Bassano and Ricci. The conclave chamber contains a retable by Carpaccio (1516).

Convento di San Giorgio (43)
isola di San Giorgio Maggiore, 30124

▥ *San Giorgio* **Giorgio Cini Foundation** ☎ *041 5289900* 🕑 *by arrangement; closed Sat., Sun.; exhibitions 10am–5.30pm; closed Mon.* ● *donations welcome; exhibitions 10,000 lire* 📋 ♿

A library, commissioned in 1433 by Cosimo de Medici, was created here by Michelozzo (but was destroyed in 1614). The buildings were reconstructed in the 15th and 16th centuries by the Buoras and by Palladio, who was still involved in the project at the time of his death. Since 1951 the convent has been used by the Cini Foundation for conferences and exhibitions.

Not forgetting

■ **Mulino Stucky (44)** Giudecca 🕑 *undergoing restoration This huge, neo-Gothic building (1895) has been in need of both restoration and a purpose since 1954.* ■ **Zitelle (45)** fondamenta delle Zitelle, Giudecca, 30133 ☎ *041 5217411* 🕑 *undergoing restoration Built to Palladio's plans and completed in 1586, its name comes from the impoverished young women who were given shelter in the nearby convent.*

44

42

41

45

In the area

Where to stay: ➡ 24 ➡ 32
Where to eat: ➡ 40 ➡ 44
After dark: ➡ 63 ➡ 66 ➡ 68
Where to shop: ➡ 140

What to see

Campo San Giacomo di Rialto (46)

▦ *Rialto*

While Piazza San Marco ➡ 78 symbolized the focus of political power, the Rialto was the commercial, banking and financial center. The headquarters of the banks, and the supervising authorities for commerce, shipping and food supply were accommodated in the Fabbriche Vecchie building, its arcades bordering the eastern side of the campo. In front of the little church of San Giacomo is the statue of the 'hunchback of the Rialto' (1541) which some saw as a symbol of the Venetian citizen crippled by taxes and dues; nearby, a pink granite column marks the spot where the Republic's decrees were read out.

Ponte di Rialto (47)

▦ *Rialto*

In 1557, it was decided that the wooden bridge spanning the Grand Canal had to be replaced by a stone bridge. The greatest architects of the time, Palladio, Vignola, Sansovino, Michelangelo, submitted their designs in competition. Eventually in 1588 the contract was awarded to Da Ponte and the bridge was built in 1591. The portico and the small shops which it shelters were later additions. Until the 19th century, the Rialto bridge was the only link between the two sides of the Grand Canal.

Campo San Bartolomio (48)

▦ *Rialto*

Pedestrians making their way to St Mark's have to walk through this square. The monument to Carlo Goldoni, the great 18th-century dramatist, was unveiled in 1883 (the bronze statue is by Dal Zotto). The church (9th century), dedicated to St Demetrius, was totally rebuilt during the 12th century; the 1723 restoration resulted in the present church which is now used as a concert hall ➡ 63.

San Salvador (49)
calle dell'Ovo, San Marco, 30124 ☎ 041 5236717

▦ *Rialto* 🕐 *9am–noon, 3.30–7pm* ● *free*

The church was completely rebuilt at the beginning of the 16th century by Giorgio Spavento, followed by Sansovino, who completed the reconstruction in 1534. Some years later, in 1569, Scamozzi provided each cupola with a lantern to remedy the lack of light. Among the interior's many funerary monuments, that of Doge Francesco Venier by Sansovino is noteworthy, as is Titian's reredos of *The Annunciation*.

Not forgetting

■ **Campo della Pescaria (50)** *Here, for the last thousand years, there has been a daily fish market. The Pescaria has survived as one of the most authentic sights of Venice.* ■ **Erbaria (51)** *The herb, fruit, vegetable and flower market still takes place every morning, alongside the Fabbriche Vecchie.*
■ **Scuola Grande di San Teodoro (52)** *calle dell'Ovo, San Marco, 30124 ☎ 041 5287227* 🕐 *opening times vary* ● *Headquarters of the Order of St Theodore, used for cultural events.*

In the area
- **Where to stay:** ➡ 24
- **Where to eat:** ➡ 46
- **After dark:** ➡ 63 ➡ 68
- **Where to shop:** ➡ 136 ➡ 138 ➡ 142

What to see

Santa Maria Gloriosa dei Frari (53)
campo dei Frari, San Polo 3072, 30125 ☎ 041 2750462

San Tomà 🕐 *9am–6pm, Sun. 1-6pm ● 3,000 lire (group tour)*

The Franciscans came to in Venice in 1220. Their first church was built during the years 1250–1330; it was demolished at the beginning of the 15th century to make way for the present basilica, completed in 1443. This pantheon of *La Serenissima*'s important personages – there are funerary monuments to several doges, to Titian and to Canova – is the city's largest church. ★ Among its treasures, the most memorable are the carved wooden choir stalls (Cozzi, 1468); *The Assumption* (1518) and the Ca' Pesaro reredos by Titian; a tryptych by G. Bellini; Paolo Veneziano's *Virgin*, and *St John the Baptist* by Donatello.

Scuola Grande di San Rocco (54)
campo San Rocco, San Polo 3054, 30125 ☎ 041 5234864

San Tomà 🕐 *Mar. 28–Nov. 2: 9am–5.30pm; Nov. 3–Mar. 27: 10am–4pm; Dec.-Feb.: 10am–1pm, Sat., Sun. 10am–4pm ● 6,000–9,000 lire* 🏧 ♿

Members of this *Scuola*, as its choice of St Roch as patron saint suggested, cared for victims of the plague; the Order entrusted Bartolomeo Bon with the building of its church and headquarters. ★ San Rocco is mainly renowned for its paintings by Tintoretto (1564–87): scenes from the life of the Virgin Mary in the lower hall, Old and New Testament subjects in the great upper hall, and allegories of the *Scuole*, a Crucifixion and scenes from the Passion in the Albergo hall.

Campo San Polo (55)

San Silvestro

This is one of Venice's largest squares and was the setting for religious celebrations and profane entertainments. It has recently reverted to a recreational role: movies are shown here as part of the Mostra ➡ 116 and it is one of the main gathering places during Carnevale ➡ 76.

San Polo (56)
campo San Polo, San Polo 1612/18, 30125 ☎ 041 2750462

San Silvestro 🕐 *10am–5pm, Sun. 1–5pm ● 3,000 lire (group tour)*

Although it has been subjected to several reconstructions, the church still retains traces of a 9th-century sanctuary (the pierced façade, fragments of cornices and pilasters flanking the entrance) and of 14th- and 15th-century additions (the wooden ceiling, rose window and side doorway). It contains paintings by Tintoretto, Veronese and Palma Giovane; the *Stations of the Cross* were painted by Giandomenico Tiepolo.

Not forgetting

■ **Casa Goldoni (57)** calle dei Nomboli, San Polo 2793, 30125
☎ 041 5236353 🕐 undergoing restoration. *Birthplace (in 1707) of Carlo Goldoni. In 1952 it was turned into a museum and center for theater studies.*
■ **San Pantalon (58)** campo San Pantalon, Dorsoduro, 30123
☎ 041 5235893 🕐 4.30–7pm, Sun. 4–7pm ● free *Worth a special visit for the spectacular decoration of the vaulted ceiling (1680–1704).*

58

54

55

53

Campo
S. Polo
55
56
Calle Magazen
C. Spezier
C. Priuli
Salizz. S. Polo
Rio di S. Polo
Canal Grande
C. 2° Saoneri
C. Saoneri
Rio terrà del Nomboli
Rio Terrà
Rio del Frari
57
C. d. Traghetto
C. S. TOMÀ
Campo
S. Tomà
S. TOMÀ
Campo
dei Frari
EX SCUOLA
D. CALEGHERI
53
Salizz. S. Rocco
Rio della Frescada
Calle larga Foscari
S. ROCCO
54
Rio della
C. d. Saoneria
Calle dei Preti
C. S.
Pantalon
Calle larga Foscari
58

53

53

Carlo Goldoni,
who transformed
Italian drama, died
in Paris in 1793.

57

In the area

➡ **Where to stay:** ➡ 26 ➡ 32
➡ **Where to eat:** ➡ 46
➡ **After dark:** ➡ 63
➡ **Where to shop:** ➡ 140 ➡ 144

What to see

Campo San Giacomo dell'Orio (59)

▦ San Stae

Off the main tourist track, this peaceful campo, with its plane trees and three 16th-century wells, epitomizes everyday, picturesque Venice. The etymology of its name is one of the most contentious: does it come from *lauro*, a bay tree that once grew in front of the church, or from *luprio*, meaning an area of firm ground in the middle of a marshy area?

San Giacomo dell'Orio (60)

campo San Giacomo dell'Orio, Santa Croce, 30135 ☎ 041 2750462

▦ San Stae 🕑 10am–5pm, Sun. 1–5pm ● 3,000 lire (group tour)

Built in the 9th and 10th centuries, this church was completely rebuilt in 1225 (the brick campanile certainly dates from that era), and altered during the late-14th–early-15th centuries. In 1549, the Chapel of the Holy Sacrament was added, to the right of the choir. The interior of the church contains works by Lorenzo Lotto, Veronese and Palma Giovane.

Fondaco dei Turchi (61)

salizzada del Fontego dei Turchi, Santa Croce 1730, 30135

▦ San Stae **Natural History Museum** ☎ 041 5240885 🕑 undergoing restoration

In 1621 the Signoria allowed Ottoman merchants to occupy this 13th-century palace. Major alterations were subsequently put in train to install 24 shops, a mosque and baths, in what became known as the Turks' Warehouse (*fondaco*) and which remained in use until 1838. In 1858, the municipality repossessed and restored it (when the flanking towers were added). In 1924 it was turned into the Natural History Museum.

Ca' Pesaro (62)

fondamenta di Ca' Pesaro, Santa Croce 2076, 30135

▦ San Stae **Museum of Modern Art** ☎ 041 721127 🕑 undergoing restoration **Museum of Oriental Art** ☎ 041 5241173 🕑 9am–2pm; closed Mon. ● 4,000 lire

This superb example of Venetian Baroque was designed by Longhena for Leonardo Pesaro. The architect died in 1682 and Antonio Gaspari completed the project in 1710. ★ In 1902 Ca' Pesaro became the Museum of Modern Art, with collections of 19th- and 20th-century works by Italian and foreign artists. Many of the exhibits in the Museum of Oriental Art, one of the most important in Europe, originally belonged to Henri de Bourbon-Parme, an ethnologist and intrepid traveler, who lived in Venice for many years.

Not forgetting

■ **Palazzo Mocenigo (63)** Santa Croce 1992, 30135 ☎ 041 721798 🕑 8.30am–1.30pm; closed Sun. ● 5,000-8,000 lire *Left to the city by Alvise Mocenigo in 1954, this palace is now the Center of Costume History, with a library and museum.* ■ **San Stae (64)** campo San Stae, Santa Croce, 30135 ☎ 041 2750462 🕑 10am–5pm, Sun. 1–5pm ● 3,000 lire (group tour). *Dedicated to St Eustace, the church was rebuilt by Giovanni Grassi at the end of the 17th century. Inside there are works by Piazzetta, Tiepolo and Ricci.*

Campo San Giacomo dell'Orio, among the loveliest of Venetian squares: the apses of the church in perfect harmony with space, the plane trees with nature.

In the area
■ **Where to stay:** ➡ 26 ➡ 30
■ **Where to eat:** ➡ 46
■ **After dark:** ➡ 66
■ **Where to shop:** ➡ 144

➡ What to see

Gli Scalzi (65)
rio terrà Lista di Spagna, Cannaregio, 30121 ☎ 041 715115

▥ Ferrovia ⊙ 7–11.45am, 4–6.45pm; Sun. 7.30am–12.30pm, 4–7pm ● free

In 1656, the religious order of the Barefoot (Scalzi) Carmelites commissioned Baldassare Longhena as architect for their church, constructed during the years 1660–80. The façade, in Carrara marble, is by Giuseppe Sardi. Tiepolo decorated the interior with frescos; one of these was destroyed by an Austrian bomb, in October 1915, but visitors can still marvel at his *Triumph of St Teresa* right side aisle, on chapel vault.

Palazzo Labia (66)
campo San Geremia, Cannaregio 275, 30121 ☎ 041 781277

▥ Ferrovia, Guglie ⊙ by arrangement: Wed.–Fri. 3–4pm ● free

Built during the late 17th and early 18th centuries by the Labia family, Catalan merchants who were admitted into the Venetian aristocracy in 1646 in return for a large contribution toward the cost of the Candia war. Nowadays this is the headquarters of RAI (Italian national television). ★ The great *salone* was decorated by Tiepolo.

San Geremia (67)
campo San Geremia, Cannaregio, 30121 ☎ 041 716181

▥ Ferrovia, Guglie ⊙ 7.30am–noon, 3–6pm ● free

The present church was built in the mid-18th century by Carlo Corbellini. The campanile, one of the oldest in Venice, dates from the 12th and 13th centuries. In the chapel to the left of the high altar, the tribune of the right transept was altered to accommodate the remains of St Lucy, moved after the demolition (for the train station) of the church that was dedicated to her. There are several Baroque altars, and Palma Giovane's *Virgin Presiding at the Coronation of Venice*.

San Simeon Grande (68)
campo San Simeon Profeta
Santa Croce, 30135 ☎ 041 718921

▥ Riva di Biasio, Ferrovia ⊙ 8am–noon, 5–6.30pm ● free

Founded in the 10th century and dedicated to the prophet St Simeon, this church was altered at the beginning of the 18th century by Domenico Margutti and again, in 1755, by Giorgio Massari. In 1861 the façade was reconstructed in neoclassical style. The interior, built on a basilical plan with three naves, contains a painting by Palma Giovane, a *Last Supper* by Tintoretto and a monument to St Simeon.

Not forgetting

■ **Ponte degli Scalzi (69)** *This stone bridge, designed by Eugenio Miozzi, was built in 1934 to replace the earlier iron bridge, erected in 1858, shortly after the construction of the first train station in 1846 (the present station dates from 1954). This is the most recent of the three bridges that span the Grand Canal.* ■ **Rio terrà Lista di Spagna (70)** *Opened in 1844, this is one of the thoroughfares that tourists have to use when going from the station to the center. It takes its name from the Spanish Embassy which used to occupy the Zeno palace (at 168, Rio terrà).*

In his frescos for the Labia palace, Tiepolo depicts ancient Egypt in terms of profligate contemporary Venetian aristocracy. Cleopatra's jewels are an allusion to the valuable collection of Maria, the wife of the *commendatore*.

In the area
- ▶ **Where to stay:** ➡ 30
- ▶ **Where to eat:** ➡ 50
- ▶ **After dark:** ➡ 66
- ▶ **Where to shop:** ➡ 144

What to see

Ghetto (71)

Guglie, San Marcuola **Museum of Jewish Art** *campo del Ghetto Nuovo, Cannaregio 2899/b, 30121 ☎ 041 715359* 🕒 *June–Sep.: 10am–7pm; Oct.–Mar.: 10am–4.30pm; closed Sat. and Jewish holidays* ● *3,000–5,000 lire* 🎧 *in Italian and English every hour 10.30am–5.30pm; other languages by prior arrangement* ● *9,000–12,000 lire* 🈯 🚫

On March 29, 1516, the Senate decided that Jews, who had lived in Venice since the end of the 14th century, were obliged to reside in the Ghetto Nuovo. Tantamount to an urban island, its only links to the rest of the city were two entrances that had to be closed at night. This decision illustrates the political pragmatism of the Venetian government: the Jews were to be allowed to stay, earning a living as pawnbrokers and dealers in second-hand clothes, while being segregated and controlled. The term *ghetto* came from the presence of a foundry (*geto*) in this district. According to the historian Brian Pullan, this lexical innovation constituted 'the Venetians' contribution to the language of persecution': *ghetto* was to become the generic term used throughout Europe to designate restricted areas for Jews (and, later, to any segregated district). From 1541 onward, the Jewish quarter grew, occupying the oldest foundries, the Ghetto Vecchio; in 1633 there was further expansion, into the Ghetto Nuovissimo. There was an extremely high population density which explains the presence of many six- or seven-story buildings, unusual for Venice. The Jews were forbidden to leave their enclave during the night and during Christian religious festivals and had to wear a distinguishing mark. They were subject to surveillance by a special magistrature. Of the nine synagogues (known as Scuole in the Venetian dialect) that existed in 1719, only five have survived: the Scuola Grande Tedesca (1528, Museum of Jewish Art), the Scuola Canton (1532, Ashkenazi rite), the Scuola Italiana (1575), the Scuola Levantina and the Scuola Spagnola (these two last being Sephardic Rite). The ghetto gates were demolished on June 10, 1797, during the French occupation of Venice 'in order that no obvious division should remain between the citizens of this city': the Austrians re-established *de facto* segregation and not until Italy was united under Victor-Emmanuel II were the Jews granted the same rights as all other Italians.

Sant'Alvise (72)
campo Sant'Alvise, Cannaregio, 30121 ☎ 041 2750462

Sant'Alvise 🕒 *undergoing restoration (group tour)*

This church was built at the end of the 14th century and dedicated to St Louis (Alvise in Venetian dialect), Bishop of Toulouse, who appeared in a dream to Antonia Venier, daughter of one of the great families of the Venetian aristocracy. The façade is Gothic but the interior, with its single nave, was altered during the 17th century. Giambattista Tiepolo worked here and the visitor can see two large canvases painted when he was a young man, *The Flagellation of Christ* and *The Crown of Thorns* (1738–40) and, in the sacristy, a remarkably assured *Ascent to Calvary*.

Not forgetting

■ **Ponte delle Guglie (73)** *This bridge owes its name to the obelisks at each end; the present stone construction (1580) replaced a wooden bridge over the Cannaregio canal, and is part of the route from the station to the Rialto.*

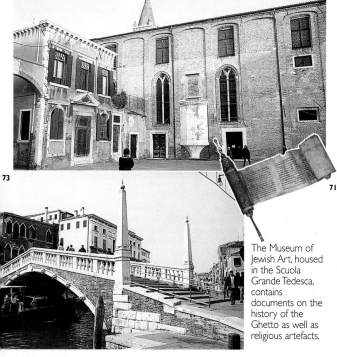

The Museum of Jewish Art, housed in the Scuola Grande Tedesca, contains documents on the history of the Ghetto as well as religious artefacts.

In the area
- Where to stay: ➡ 19 ➡ 32
- Where to eat: ➡ 50
- After dark: ➡ 70
- Where to shop: ➡ 140 ➡ 144

What to see

Madonna dell'Orto (74)
campo Madonna dell'Orto
Cannaregio, 30121 ☎ 041 2750462

▦ Madonna dell'Orto ◷ 10am–5pm, Sun.1–5pm ● 3,000 lire (group tour)

Begun at the end of the 14th century, the church was completed a century later. The Gothic façade in red brick is decorated with statues of the twelve apostles; the doorway is typical of the transitional period between Gothic and Renaissance. ★ The interior bears witness to the genius of Tintoretto. He painted the *Last Judgment* and *The Worship of the Golden Calf* (chancel), *The Martyrdom of St Christopher* and the *Apparition of the Cross to St Peter* (apse), *The Presentation of the Virgin Mary in the Temple* (chapel of right apse). The church also contains other masterpieces, among them is a *St John the Baptist* by Cima da Conegliano, painted during his sojourn in Venice (end of 15th century), a *Virgin with Child* by Giovanni Bellini (1478). Near the church stands the Scuola dei Mercanti (1570), whose superb collection of paintings (Veronese, Tintoretto) was 'lost' during the Napoleonic occupation.

Campo dell'Abazia (75)

▦ Fondamente Nove

In this square, which, like the Campo Madonna dell'Orto, has retained its chevron-brick paving, stand the ancient church of Santa Maria della Misericordia, the Scuola Vecchia and the Scuola Nuova della Misericordia. Off the beaten tourist track, near the 'empty quarter' of Venice, this deserted area of the northern lagoon known as the Sacca della Misericordia, peaceful and picturesque, is well worth a detour.

Santa Maria della Misericordia (76)
campo dell'Abazia, Cannaregio, 30121

▦ Fondamente Nove ◷ temporarily closed

Founded in the 10th century on what was then Valverde Island, this church was altered during the 13th century. The façade, with statues by Clemente Moli of Bologna, was built during the years 1651–9, at the expense of the aristocrat Gasparo Moro (whose portrait appears on the façade). The Scuola Vecchia della Misericordia, which abuts the Gothic church, was once decorated with sculptures by Bartolomeo Bon; these are now in the Victoria and Albert Museum in London. A short distance away, beyond the bridge, is the Scuola Nuova, built by Sansovino in 1534 at the behest of the Misericordia religious order – who had sold their original headquarters to the corporation of silk weavers. Fifty years were to pass before the interior was completed and the exterior is still unfinished.

Not forgetting

■ **Campo dei Mori (77)** *Owes its name to three statues (late 13th century); popular tradition sees in them the three Levantine merchants of the Mastelli family.* ■ **Palazzo Contarini dal Zaffo (78)** fondamenta Gasparo Contarini, Cannaregio 3539, 30121 *Built during the 16th century in a magnificent park that looked out over the Sacca della Misericordia; in these gardens and in the Casino degli spiriti (the 'Pavilion of the Spirits') Aretino and Titian participated in the discussions that took place on literary and artistic subjects.*

74

76

78

The statue in Campo dei Mori, disfigured by an ugly iron nose, was nicknamed Sior Antonio Rioba in whose name lampoons expressing popular discontent were circulated.

In the area
▸ **Where to stay:** ➡ 32
▸ **Where to eat:** ➡ 52
▸ **After dark:** ➡ 61 ➡ 66
▸ **Where to shop:** ➡ 140

What to see

Ca' d'Oro (79)
calle di Ca' d'Oro, Cannaregio 3932, 30131

Ca' d'Oro **Franchetti Gallery** ☎ 041 5238790 ⏱ 9am–2pm ● 6,000 lire

This palace is a superb example of Venetian Gothic, built for Marino Contarini by Bartolomeo and Giovanni Bon. It owes its name (The Golden House) to the gilding that originally adorned the façade. At the end of the 19th century, it was purchased and restored by a musician and art collector, Giorgio Franchetti who donated the palace and his collections to the State in 1916. Exhibits in the museum include works by Carpaccio, Titian and Mantegna as well as exceptionally fine furniture, Flemish tapestries and a collection of medals.

San Marcuola (80)
campo San Marcuola, Cannaregio, 30121 ☎ 041 713872

San Marcuola ⏱ 9.30am–noon, 5–6.30pm; Sun. no visits allowed ● free

This church is dedicated to St Ermagora and St Fortunatus: Marcuola is thought to be a corruption of these names. Founded around the year 1000, the church was rebuilt in the 12th century, based on a basilical plan, and altered during the 18th century. At the same time, the façade, looking onto the Grand Canal, was designed by Massari but never completed. Inside the church is Tintoretto's *Last Supper* (1547).

Ca' Vendramin Calergi (81)
campiello Vendramin, Cannaregio 2040, 30121 ☎ 041 5297111

San Marcuola **Municipal Casino** ➡ 61 ⏱ 3pm–2.30am ● 10,000 lire

★ This majestic palace, designed by Mauro Codussi for the Loredan family, completed at the beginning of the 16th century, is a Renaissance gem. In 1589 it passed into the hands of the powerful Calergi family (who came from Crete) and then to their cousins, the Vendramin. In 1844 it was acquired by the Duchess of Berry. Wagner spent the last months of his life in this palace and died here on February 13, 1883. It was purchased by the Municipality of Venice in 1946 and turned into a winter casino.

Santa Maria Maddalena (82)
campo della Maddalena, Cannaregio, 30121 ☎ 041 713872

San Marcuola, Ca' d'Oro ⏱ Sun., church festivals 8am–6pm ● free

Founded in the 13th century by the Balbo family, the church was rebuilt (1760–89) in neoclassical style by Tommaso Temanza. The exterior, of circular construction, and its dome were inspired by the Pantheon in Rome; the interior is based on a hexagonal plan, off which lead four chapels.

Not forgetting

■ **Strada Nova (83)** *The only 'street' in Venice. Its construction in 1871 to link the train station with the Rialto necessitated the demolition of many buildings in the Cannaregio sestiere: the street still seems alien in the Venetian townscape.*
■ **Campo Santa Fosca (84)** *In the middle of this campo stands a statue of Friar Paolo Arpi (1552–1623), an opponent of Pope Paul II who had issued interdicts against the Serenissima in 1606.*

80

Map showing:
- Rio terra Cietro la Chiesa — **80**
- Rio dei Servi
- Rio terra della Maddalena
- **81**
- PALAZZO EMO
- **82**
- **84** S. FOSCA
- Strada Nova
- PAL. GUSSONI GRIMANI
- Rio di Noale
- Campo S. Felice
- S. FELICE
- **83** Fond d. Chiesa
- Rio di S. Felice
- **79**
- Strada Nova
- C. di Ca' d'Oro
- PALAZZO SAGREDO
- Canal Grande

83

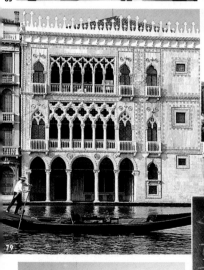

79

82

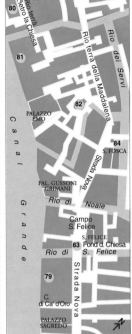

84

79

Mantegna's *St Sebastian* is indubitably the most famous of all the paintings in the Ca' d'Oro Museum.

81

In the area
- ◗ **Where to stay:** ➡ 32
- ◗ **Where to eat:** ➡ 52 ➡ 54
- ◗ **After dark:** ➡ 62
- ◗ **Where to shop:** ➡ 140

What to see

Santi Apostoli (85)
campo dei Santi Apostoli, Cannaregio, 30131 ☎ 041 5238297

▦ *Ca' d'Oro* ◷ *7.30–11.30am, 3–6.30pm* ● *free*

The foundations of this church may date from as early as the 9th century; it was rebuilt in 1575, and underwent several alterations, its present appearance being the result of 18th-century restoration by the architect Giovanni Pedolo. The interior, with its single nave, retains the 16th-century structure; the Corner chapel, attributed to Mauro Codussi, also dates from this period and contains Veronese's *The Fall of Manna* and a small reredos by Tiepolo, *The Communion of St Lucy*.

I Gesuiti (86)
campo dei Gesuiti, Cannaregio, 30131

▦ *Fondamente Nove* **Oratory** ☎ 041 5217411 ◷ *Apr.–Oct.: Fri.–Sun. 10am–1pm; closed Mon.–Thu.* ● *3,000 lire* **Church** ☎ 041 5286579 ◷ *10am–noon, 4–6pm* ● *free*

The oratory of the Crociferi (the order of the 'Bearers of the Cross') which had occupied this site from the 12th century, was rebuilt in the 16th century, after a fire. In the years 1583–91 Palma Giovane, completed a cycle of paintings illustrating great moments in the order's history. Accused of leading dissolute lives, the order was suppressed in 1656 by Pope Alexander VII. After the Jesuits returned to Venice after their fifty-year banishment (they had been exiled from Venice at the time of the quarrel between the Serene Republic and Pope Paul V, in 1606), they repurchased the oratory in 1657. The church of Santa Maria Assunta was completely rebuilt during the period 1715–29, by the architect Domenico Rossi. ★ The interior is remarkable for its Baroque exuberance; among the masterpieces here are Tintoretto's *Assumption* and Titian's reredos *The Martyrdom of St Laurence* (1588).

Santa Maria dei Miracoli (87)
campo dei Miracoli, Cannaregio, 30131 ☎ 041 2750462

▦ *Rialto* ◷ *10am–5pm, Sun. 1–5pm* ● *3,000 lire (group tour)*

This 'precious Renaissance jewel' was built during the years 1481–89 by Pietro Lombardo to contain the miraculous image of the *Virgin and Child* Nicolò di Pietro (1408; high altar). Both the exterior and interior of the building are covered in polychrome marble, like a marquetry jewel box: ★ the façade is adorned with medallions and panels in porphyry and green marble, the interior with marble in delicate shades of pink, silvery gray and white. There is a very ornate choir gallery above a sort of crypt, and a barrel-vaulted ceiling decorated with fifty painted panels of prophets and patriarchs.

Not forgetting

■ **San Canziano (88)** campiello Bruno Crovato (già San Canzian), Cannaregio, 30131 ☎ 041 5235293 ◷ *7.30am–noon, 5.30–7.30pm* ● *free* *Founded in the 9th century, the church has been frequently altered over the centuries; the façade dates from the 18th century. Inside, the Widmann chapel is worthy of note, built by Longhena and decorated by Clemente Moli in sumptuous Baroque style.*

86

87

86

Doge Pasquale Cicogna at Priamo Balbi's Mass, Palma Giovane. When commissioned to decorate the oratory of the Order of Cross-Bearers, the young painter achieved his finest work.

The campanile of Santi Apostoli, one of the highest in Venice, has a tiny shop at ground level.

86

87

85

In the area
 Where to stay: ➡ 20 ➡ 32
 Where to eat: ➡ 54
 After dark: ➡ 63
 Where to shop: ➡ 132

What to see

Santi Giovanni e Paolo (89)
campo Santi Giovanni e Paolo, Castello, 30122 ☎ 041 5235913

▪ Ospedale Civile ⏱ 8am–12.30pm, 3.30–6pm; Sun.: no visits allowed ● free

The Dominicans started to build this church toward the end of the 13th century. The façade is a fine example of 14th-century Gothic: the great doorway is later (1458), and is an early example of the transition from Gothic to Renaissance. Like the Frari, its Franciscan 'rival' ➡ 96, the church is the last resting place of the Most Serene Republic's luminaries: twenty-five doges are buried here, as well as *condottieri* and artists (Lotto, Bellini). ★ Among the masterpieces in the church are: the polyptych of *St Vincent Ferrier* by G. Bellini (c. 1465); *St Antoninus Giving Alms* by Lotto (mid-16th century). In pride of place in this campo, usually referred to as Campo Zanipolo, a contraction of the two Roman martyrs' names, is the statue of a *condottiere* from Bergamo, Bartolomeo Colleoni, Captain-General of the Venetian armies in the 15th century.

Scuola Grande di San Marco (90)
campo Santi Giovanni e Paolo, Castello, 30122 ☎ 041 5294111

▪ Ospedale Civile ⏱ 8.30am–12.30pm; closed Sun., public holidays ● free

The charitable institution, founded in 1260, has occupied this site in campo Zanipolo since 1437. The present building, which replaced an earlier one destroyed by fire, is by Pietro Lombardo and Giovanni Buora, but was completed by Mauro Codussi at the end of the 15th century. On the first floor, despite the dispersal of many of the original contents, there remains a large number of works by Palma Vecchio, Domenico Tintoretto (Tintoretto's son) and Giovanni Mansueti.

Santa Maria Formosa (91)
campo Santa Maria Formosa, Castello 5263
30122 ☎ 041 2750462

▪ San Zaccaria ⏱ 10am–5pm, Sun. 1–5pm ● 3,000 lire (group tour)

In 1492, on foundations dating from the 11th century, Mauro Codussi designed a building on a Latin cross plan, with three naves. In 1542 the aristocratic Cappello family commissioned the main façade, followed in 1604 by the façade giving onto the square. The church contains paintings by Bartolomeo Vivarini (Triptych, 1473), the two Palmas, and Giambattista Tiepolo. Numerous *scuole* and corporations had their own chapels and altars in the church.

Fondazione Querini Stampalia (92)
campiello Querini Stampalia, Castello 4778
30122 ☎ 041 2711411

▪ San Zaccaria **Art Gallery** ⏱ Tue.–Thu., Sun. 10am–1pm, 3–6pm, Fri., Sat.: 10am–1pm, 3–10pm; closed Mon. ● 8,000–12,000 lire 🎫 by arrangement 🏛
▪ 🔖 **Library** ⏱ 4–11.30pm, Sat. 2.30–11.30pm, Sun. 3–6pm ● free

This Renaissance palace, which curves round a bend in the canal, was bequeathed to the city by the last descendant of the Querini-Stampalia family. ★ The building, restored in 1959–63 by Carlo Scarpa, contains a splendid library and an art gallery with the series of paintings by Gabriel Bella of scenes from everyday life in 18th-century Venice.

89

Map labels:
- C. larga G. Gallina
- della Testa
- Rio dei Mendicanti
- C.po SS. Giov. e Paolo
- Salizz. SS. Giov. e Paolo
- Calle
- C. delle Erbe
- C. d. Cavallo
- Bressana
- Madonna
- C. d. Venier
- Fond. Felzi
- Rio di San Marina
- Campo S. Marina
- Calle Pindemonte
- C. di Borgoloco
- C. d. Dose
- PALAZZO DONA
- Calle Trevisana
- C. Piombo
- PALAZZO RUZZINI
- Campo S. Maria Formosa
- C. d. Nave
- C. d. Volto
- C. d. Paradiso
- Salizzada
- Ramo d. Malvasia
- Calle S. Antonio
- S. Lio
- C. Mondo Nuovo
- C. d. Bande
- PALAZZO AVOGADRO
- **90**
- **89**
- **91**
- **92**

91

89

90

92

In the area
➜ Where to stay: ➡ 18 ➡ 34
➜ Where to eat: ➡ 56
➜ After dark: ➡ 63
➜ Where to shop: ➡ 132

What to see

Scuola di San Giorgio degli Schiavoni (93)
calle dei Furlani, Castello, 30122 ☎ 041 5228828

🚇 *Pietà, San Zaccaria* 🕐 Apr.–Sep.: 9.30am–12.30pm, 3.30–6.30pm, Sun. 9am–12.30pm; Oct.–Mar.: 10am–12.30pm, 3–6pm, Sun. 10am–12.30pm; closed Mon. ● 5,000 lire

Dalmatians (*schiavoni*), mainly sailors and artisans, started to settle in Venice in the 14th century; they organized themselves into a Scuola, the statutes of which were approved by the Council of Ten in 1451. ★ At the end of the 15th century, the confraternity erected their first premises and commissioned nine paintings from Carpaccio illustrating the lives of the three patron saints of Dalmatia (George, Tryphon and Jerome as recounted in the *Golden Legend* by Brother Voragine, a Dominican from Genoa.

San Francesco della Vigna (94)
campo della Confraternita, Castello, 30122 ☎ 041 5206102

🚇 *Celestia* 🕐 8am–12.30pm, 3–7pm ● free

The name no doubt refers to the vines once cultivated on land given in 1253 to the Franciscans who built a church and a monastery here. The church contains Veronese's reredos *The Sacred Conversation*. Situated between the church and the lagoon, the monastery, with its three cloisters, provides a fine example of 14th-century Gothic architecture.

San Zaccaria (95)
campo San Zaccaria, Castello, 30122 ☎ 041 5221257

🚇 *San Zaccaria* 🕐 10am–noon, 4–6pm ● free

Founded at the beginning of the 9th century, the church acquired its present appearance when it was rebuilt between 1453 and 1543. ★ Inside, the reredos of *The Sacred Conversation* (1505) is by Giovanni Bellini, the frescos are by Andrea del Castagno and altar paintings by Antonio Vivarini and his brother-in-law, Giovanni d'Alemagna (1442–44).

San Giovanni in Bragora (96)
campo Bandiera e Moro, Castello, 30122 ☎ 041 5205906

🚇 *Arsenale* 🕐 8.30–11am, 3–5pm, Sat. 3–5pm; closed Sun. ● free

The earliest records of this church's existence date back to 1090; work began on the present exterior in 1475; the interior was altered in the 18th century. ★ Interesting contents include works by Alvise Vivarini, Cima da Conegliano and Palma Giovane, as well as Vivaldi's baptismal certificate ➡ 63.

Not forgetting

■ **San Giorgio dei Greci (97)** campo dei Greci, Castello, 30122 ☎ 041 5225446 🕐 10am–noon, 3–5pm ● free *There were Greeks living in Venice from the 11th century. After the fall of Constantinople, in 1453, they sought refuge in Venice in great numbers. In 1526 the Greek community obtained authorization to celebrate the Orthodox rite and entrusted the construction of their church to Sante Lombardo.*
■ **Museo dei dipinti sacri bizantini (98)** ponte dei Greci, Castello 3412, 30122 ☎ 041 5226581 🕐 9am–12.30pm, 1.30–4.30pm; Sun. 10am–5pm ● 4,000–7,000 lire *One of Europe's finest collections of Byzantine icons.*

98

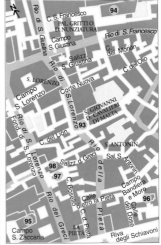

95

94

95

96

In the area

▪ **Where to stay:** ➡ 34
▪ **Where to eat:** ➡ 56
▪ **After dark:** ➡ 63
▪ **Where to shop:** ➡ 132

➡ What to see

Arsenale (99)

▦ *Arsenale* ◷ *during exhibitions only* ● *varies*

From the outset Venice's power was underpinned by consummate mastery of the art of shipbuilding. The exact date of the construction of the first arsenal is not known, but it is beyond question that as early as the beginning of the 13th century a depot for armaments, oars, rigging and material for the building and repair of galleys already existed. The shipbuilding industry still relied, however, on the private initiative of the *squeri*. Only after 1320 was a state arsenal built for the construction of galleys, with *arsenalotti* working in teams. During this period (early 14th century) depots and factories were also erected for the storage and manufacture of ropes, such as La Tana — where some of the Art Biennale exhibitions now take place. The monumental entrance to the Arsenal (1460) has the appearance of a triumphal arch, surmounted by a tympanum with a carved Lion of St Mark, attributed to Bartolomeo Bon.

Biennale Internazionale d'Arte (100)
Giardini Pubblici, Castello, 30122 ☎ 041 5218711

▦ *Giardini* ◷ *pavilions open during exhibitions: 9am–6pm* ● *varies*
@ dae@labiennale.com

The first art exhibition was opened on April 30, 1895 by King Umberto and Queen Margherita. In an area of the Public Gardens (laid out at the beginning of the 19th century by Gianantonio Selva) reserved for the Biennale, pavilions are erected: these are often designed by well-known architects, and thus provide an interesting insight into architectural trends; Joseph Hoffman designed the Austrian pavilion (1934), Gerrit-Thomas Rietveld that of the Netherlands (1954), Carlo Scarpa the Venezuelan pavilion (1956) and the Finnish pavilion is by Alvar Aato (1956), while James Stirling designed the Book Pavilion (1991).

San Pietro di Castello (101)
campo San Pietro, Castello, 30122 ☎ 041 2750462

▦ *San Pietro, Giardini* ◷ *10am–5pm, Sun. 1–5pm* ● *3,000 lire (group tour)*

St Peter's church used to be the seat of the Archbishop of Venice and, from 1451, of the Patriarch, but in 1807 the distinction was conferred on St Mark's. The present building (1596) is the work of Francesco Smeraldi and Giangirolamo Grapiglia, disciples of Palladio.

Not forgetting

■ **Muso storico navale (102)** campo San Biagio, Castello 2148, 30122 ☎ 041 5200276 ◷ 8.45am–1.30pm, Sat. 8.45am–1pm; closed Sun.
● 3,000 lire. *The forerunner of this Museum of Naval History was the 'house of models' where, during the 17th century, the Venetian government kept models of ships built in the city's shipyards. Here the visitor can see navigational instruments, uniforms, models of Venetian fortresses in the Mediterranean, scale models of various types of craft, including a Bucentaur ➡ 76.*
■ **La Marinaressa (103)** riva dei Sette Martiri, Castello, 30122
These lodgings were built during the 15th and 16th centuries as quarters for the Republic's sailors and the arsenalotti.

Since 1692, the entrance to the Arsenale has been 'guarded' by two lions, war booty brought back from Athens, after the reconquest of Morea in 1687 by Francesco Morosini.

99

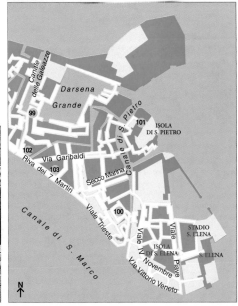

Darsena Grande

Canale delle Galeazze

Canale di S. Pietro

ISOLA DI S. PIETRO

99

101

102

Via Garibaldi

Riva dei 7 Martiri

103

Secco Marina

100

Viale Trieste

Viale IV Novembre

Viale Piave

Canale di S. Marco

ISOLA DI S. ELENA

STADIO S. ELENA

S. ELENA

V.le Vittorio Veneto

N

01

100

99

In the area
▪▶ **Where to stay:** ➡ 36
▪▶ **Where to eat:** ➡ 58
▪▶ **After dark:** ➡ 61
▪▶ **Where to shop:** ➡ 146

➡ **What to see**

Lido (104)

▦ Lido, San Nicolò

No sooner had its immense beaches of fine sand been discovered in the mid-19th century than the Lido became the most fashionable resort on the Adriatic coast, patronized by artists and aristocrats from all over Europe. This was when the luxury hotels in Art-Nouveau style were built ➡ 36. During the 1930s, the summer Casino was built ➡ 61 and the headquarters of the movie festival, La Mostra (first held in August 1932).

Murano (105)

▦ Museo **Basilica** ☎ 041 739056 🕙 8am–noon, 4–7pm ● free **Glass Museum** ☎ 041 739586 🕙 Apr.–Oct: 10am–5pm; Nov.–Mar.: 10am–4pm; closed Wed. ● 5,000–8,000 lire; Venice Municipal Museums ticket valid

This is the largest island in the lagoon, less than a mile from Venice. The island owes its prosperity to glassmaking, relocated here at the end of the 13th century because of fire risks. The Glass Museum, installed in the late-17th-century Palazzo Giustiniani in 1861, charts the highlights of Murano's glass industry and also exhibits contemporary glassware ➡ 146. ★ The Basilica di Santa Maria e San Donato, reliably thought to have been founded in the 7th century, was rebuilt during the 12th century, after the relics of St. Donatus had been brought here from Cephalonia, in 1125. The influence of Roman art is discernible in the remarkable apse facing the water and that of Byzantine art on the interior, in the marble mosaic floor.

Burano (106)

▦ Burano **Lace museum** ☎ 041 730034 🕙 10am–5pm; closed Tue. ● 5,000–8,000 lire; Venice Municipal Museums ticket valid

Burano looks very different from the other islands: here there are no imposing palaces, no majestic churches but, instead, a certain uniformity with houses very similar in size, all painted in bright colors. From the 16th century onward, the island's name was associated with needlepoint lace, long one of the most highly prized Venetian craft products. Genuine Burano lace is now a luxury (a tablecloth takes ten craftswomen three years to make!) and the last remaining lacemakers still using traditional techniques believe that their art will die with them.

Torcello (107)

▦ Torcello **Cathedral** ☎ 041 730084 🕙 10am–5pm ● 3,000–5,000 lire **Museo dell'Estuario** ☎ 041 730761 🕙 10am–12.30pm, 2–5.30pm, Sun. 10.30am–12.30pm; closed Mon., public holidays ● 1,500–3,000 lire

This lonely island in the middle of the lagoon was once the departure point for the settlement of the lagoon and the most powerful member of the confederation which gave birth to the Venetian State. Torcello's power waned as Venice grew and its decline accelerated in the 15th and 16th centuries. ★ Some relics of its former glory remain: a remarkable group of ecclesiastical buildings: the cathedral of Santa Maria Assunta (9th, 11th centuries), with mosaics in the Veneto-Byzantine style (apses), a vast *Last Judgment* (11th–13th centuries) and a fine floor of marble mosaic. The church of Santa Fosca (11th–12th centuries) is octagonal, girdled by a portico with stilted arches resting on pillars with Veneto-Byzantine capitals.

107

104

105

106

Further afield

Palladian villas

Unless you can get there by boat, the 'Padana Superiore' main road (route 11) connecting Padua and Vicenza, which follows the course of the Brenta, is the best way to discover the magnificent Palladian villas built on the banks of the waterway ➡ 124.

Fortified towns of the Veneto region

Not far from Venice, between Treviso and Padua, are two of the finest fortified towns of the Veneto region: **Castelfranco Veneto**, birthplace of the painter Giorgione, and **Cittadella**, the walls of which form an elegant oval.

Sea or mountain?

A regular ferry service (ACTV ☎ 041 5287886 @ www.actv.it) connects Venice with **Lido di Jesolo**, one of the most popular resorts on the Adriatic coast. Mountain lovers can easily reach resorts in the **Dolomites** by train or bus from Mestre.

18 Days out

The area around Treviso

Treviso, a fine old town, less than a half-hour by train from Venice, is a good starting point for visiting a region rich in natural beauty and works of art. Of special interest is **Asolo**, where Caterina Cornaro, queen of Cyprus, made her home. More recent residents have been the English poet Robert Browning and the actress Eleonora Duse. In the hills near Asolo, at **Maser**, it is possible to visit the *Villa Barbaro Volpi* ☎ 0423923004, designed by Palladio and decorated with frescos by Veronese.

The Euganean Hills

Starting from Padua ➡ 126, it is possible to plan a delightful itinerary taking in the famous thermal resorts of **Abano** and **Montegrotto** and a number of historic centers perched on the gentle slopes of the Euganean Hills, for instance **Arquà Petrarca**, a small medieval town where the poet Petrarch spent his retirement (you can visit his house). Not far away is *Praglia Abbey* ☎ 0499900010, the home since 1904 of a group of Benedictine monks who restore manuscripts and antique books.

Venice inevitably overshadows its neighbors (Padua, Vicenza…) but a good network of state highways and expressways means that these important places are only a half-hour away from the City of the Doges and it is worth spending at least a day in each of them.

Further afield

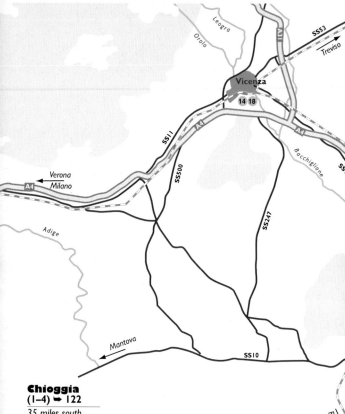

Chioggia
(1–4) ➡ 122

35 miles south
🚌 SS 309 'Strada Romea' toward Ferrara (1 hr 30 mins)

🚊🚌🚊 (line 6) Piazza San Marco-Lido, then bus line 11 Lido (Santa Maria Elisabetta)-Pellestrina, then ferryboat line 11 M/N Pellestrina-Chioggia (1 hr 30 mins) ACTV
☎ 041 5287886
● 8,000 lire, 15,000 lire round trip

Riviera del Brenta (5–8)
➡ 124

20 miles west
🚊 'Il Burchiello' boat cruise up the Brenta Canal, visiting Palladian villas (9 hrs 30 mins) New Siamic Express
☎ 049660944
➡ 049662830
🗓 Apr.–Oct.: Tue., Thu., Sat.; leaves 9am from Pietà pontoon, on Riva degli Schiavoni, Castello, and arrives 6.30pm at Padua train station
● Apr. 1–June 3 and Sep. 1–Oct. 30: 65,000–110,000 lire; July 4–Aug. 31: 65,000–99,000 lire; not including admission to Villa Pisani. 43,000 lire for lunch (optional)

Villa Pisani
(5) ➡ 124

21 miles west (Stra)
🚌 SS 11 toward Padua (40 mins)
🚊 Venice-Padua intercity line (55 mins) ACTV
☎ 041 5287886
● 4,500 lire, 8,500 lire round trip

Villa Foscarini Rossi (6) ➡ 124

21 miles west (Stra)
🚌 SS 11 en toward Padua (40 mins)

🚆 Venice-Padua intercity line (55 mins) ACTV
☎ 041 5287886
● 4,500 lire, 8,500 lire round trip

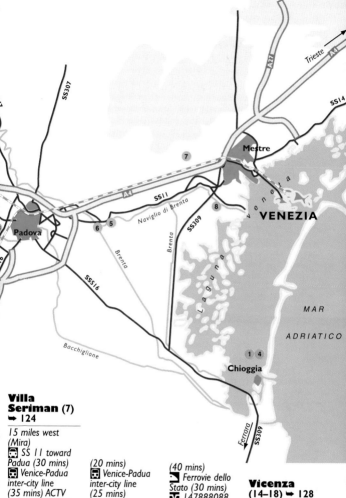

Villa Seriman (7) ➡ 124

15 miles west (Mira)
🚌 SS 11 toward Padua (30 mins)
🚆 Venice-Padua inter-city line (35 mins) ACTV
☎ 041 5287886
● 3,000 lire, 5,500 lire round trip

Villa Foscari (8) ➡ 124

10 miles west (Malcontenta)
🚌 SS 11 toward Padua

(20 mins)
🚆 Venice-Padua inter-city line (25 mins)
☎ 041 5287886
● 3,000 lire, 5,500 lire round trip

Padua (9–13) ➡ 126

20 miles west
🚗 A4 'Serenissima', Padua Est exit

(40 mins)
🚆 Ferrovie dello Stato (30 mins)
Ⓥ 147888088
● 12,300 lire (1st class), 8,200 lire (2nd class)
🚆 Venice-Padua intercity line 1 hr 15 mins ACTV
☎ 041 5287886
● 6,000 lire, 10,000 lire round trip

Vicenza (14–18) ➡ 128

34 miles west
🚗 A4 'Serenissima', Vicenza Est exit (1 hr)
🚆 Ferrovie dello Stato (52 mins)
☎ 147888088
● 15,400 lire (1st class), 9,400 lire (2nd class)

Barbarian invasions forced the people of the Venetian hinterland to take refuge on the islands in the lagoon, Chioggia soon fell under the sway of Venice but this did not hinder its mercantile development. Since 1921 it has been linked to the mainland by a bridge but retains the charm of a Venice in miniature; along the narrow streets, the dialect that Goldoni immortalized in

Further afield

Duomo (1)
corso del Popolo, 30015 ☎ 041400496

🕐 10am–noon, Sat. 10am–noon, 3–6pm, Sun. 10am–6pm ● free

The present cathedral, built in Palladian style, was probably Baldassare Longhena's first important commission. He designed the cathedral after a fire had destroyed its predecessor in 1623. A classically inspired portal is set in the unfinished façade, while against the right-hand outside wall there are 15th-century sculptures of the Virgin Mary surrounded by saints that have survived from the original building, as has the fountain set against the left hand wall. ★ From the top of the bell tower (1347–50) there are wonderful panoramic views over the town and the lagoon. The chapel of St Felix and St Fortunatus (1729), is noteworthy for its series of paintings.

Santa Trinità (2)
corso del Popolo, 30015 ☎ 041400513

🕐 undergoing restoration

The original building, known as the Rossi church, was built in 1528. It was rebuilt in 1703 to the designs of Andrea Tirali who gave it a very simple brick façade, with a Renaissance portal. The interior, in the shape of a Greek cross, is adorned with Corinthian columns and has a central cupola; behind the high altar is the entrance to the oratory (this was once the church of the Battuti Order of Flagellants); there are some fine paintings by Palma Giovane and various other Venetian late Mannerists.

Corso del Popolo (3)

Dating from the 18th century, this runs from one end of Chioggia to the other, alongside the Vena canal and is the town's main thoroughfare, on which numerous small streets, running parallel with one another, converge. The most important civil and religious buildings face onto this street. Half-way along it, under the arcades of the grain market (the Granaio), is a single story building where a market is held daily.

San Domenico (4)
isola di San Domenico, 30015 ☎ 041400757

🕐 8am–noon, 2.30–5.30pm ● free

The church is situated on the island of the same name. Founded in the 18th century, at the same time as the adjoining monastery, for a religious order that was dissolved in 1770, the church was rebuilt between 1745 and 1762. The bell tower, with its gemeled window revealing the clock inside, was built in the 14th century. ★ Worth a detour for the works of art including a *Deposition* by Leandro Bassano, a painting attributed to Tintoretto and a *St. Paul*, the last known work of Carpaccio (1520).

Not forgetting

■ **El Gato** campo Sant'Andrea 653, 30015 ☎ 041401806 🕐 noon– 2.30pm, 7–10.30pm; closed lunch Mon., Tue., and Jan.–mid. Feb. *Regional cooking.*
■ **Antica Pasticceria Ciosota** calle Garibaldi 123, 30015 ☎ 041401544 🕐 8am–1pm, 3–7.30pm; closed Mon. *Cakes and cookies typical of this area.*

his *Le Baruffe Chiozzotte* can still be heard today.

The colors of the lateen sails of Chioggia's fishing craft denote membership of the fishermen's associations.

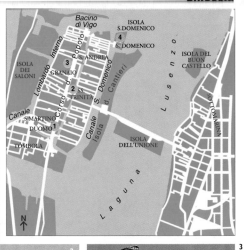

4

During the 15th century, wishing to improve links with Padua, the Venetian authorities embarked upon the construction of the Brenta Canal (opened in 1442) in one of the River Brenta's two former river beds. On both banks, Venetian aristocrats built sumptuous summer residences, easily reached by gondola.

Further afield

Villa Pisani Nazionale (5)
via Doge Pisani 7, Stra, 30039 ☎ 049 9800590

🕐 *Apr.–Oct.: 9am–6pm; Nov.–Mar.: 9am–4pm* ● *10,000 lire (villa and gardens), 5,000 lire (gardens only)*

Designed for the Pisani family by Frigimelica around 1720, the villa was completed in the late 1730s by Francesco Maria Preti. ★ The ballroom was decorated with frescos in 1761–62 by Tiepolo. Sold in 1807 to Napoleon who gave it to Eugène de Beauharnais, the villa passed into the hands of the Hapsburgs in 1815 and, in 1866, into the ownership of the House of Savoy. It now belongs to the Italian State. In the fine park, where visitors can explore the maze (1721) described by D'Annunzio in *The Fire*, there are hothouses, an orangery, and some elegant stables.

Villa Foscarini Rossi (6)
via Doge Pisani 1, Stra, 30039 ☎ 049 9801091

🕐 *Mar.–Oct.: 9am–noon, 2.30–6pm; Sat., Sun. 10am–6pm; closed Mon.; Nov.–Feb.: 9am–noon, 2–6pm; closed Sat. and Sun.* ● *4,000–6,000 lire*

Attributed to Scamozzi, the house was built during the years 1586–1605 for the Foscarini family. It was restored during the 19th century by Giuseppe Jappelli, who changed the layout of the gardens. The present owner, the shoe manufacturer Rossimoda, has opened a museum of luxury shoes from 1950 to the present day, as well as a modern art gallery.

Villa Seriman (7)
via Nazionale 420, Mira, 30034 ☎ 041 424156

🕐 *Apr.–May and Oct.: 10am–5pm; June–Sep. 10am–6pm; closed Mon.* ● *8,000 lire* **Barchesse Valmarana** ☎ *041 5102341* 🕐 *9am–12.30pm, 2.30–5.30pm; closed Mon.* ● *8,000 lire*

Built in 1719 for the Seriman family, this property passed through the ownership of several families before it was purchased by the provincial government. Its present Rococo appearance resulted from mid-18th-century alterations. The interior's frescos have been attributed to Giuseppe Angeli. ★ The outbuildings of the 17th-century Villa Valmarana, demolished in 1908, can be seen on the other side of the canal.

Villa Foscari (8)
via dei Turisti 10, Malcontenta, 30030 ☎ 041 5470012

🕐 *Apr.–Nov. 15: Tue., Sat. 9am–noon; Wed.–Fri. and Sun. by arrangement; closed Mon.* ● *12,000 lire, 15,000 for visits by arrangement*

This villa, built by Palladio around 1555, was also known as 'La Malcontenta' after the unfaithful wife of a Foscari was exiled here. ★ The finest façade has a loggia with Ionic columns and faces onto the river. The decoration of the interiors, (1561), is the work of Giambattista Zelotti and Battista Franco.

Not forgetting

■ **Margherita** via Nazionale 312, Mira, 30030 ☎ 041 420879 🕐 noon–3.30pm, 7–10.30pm; closed Tue. evening, Wed., Jan. *Excellent fish dishes.*
■ **Nalin** via Novissimo, Mira, 30030 ☎ 041 420083 🕐 noon–2pm, 7.30–10.15pm; closed Sun. evening, Mon. *Good cooking from the Veneto region.*

VILLA
FOSCARINI
STRA
VILLA
PISANI
6 5
DOLO
Naviglio di Brenta
ORIAGO
VILLA
SERIMAN 7
MIRA
VILLA
VALMARANA
Naviglio di Brenta
VILLA
FOSCARI
8
N

5

5

8

7

6

Rome claims to trace its origins back to Aeneas, but Padua is equally illustrious: legend has it that the city was founded in 1182 BC by Antenor, another Trojan hero who escaped the torching of his native city. Padua was prosperous and powerful throughout the Middle Ages; the founding of the great university (1222) and St Anthony's preaching

Further afield

Piazza delle Erbe (9)

Palazzo della Ragione ☎ 049 8205006 🕙 9am–7pm; closed Mon. ● 7,000 lire

This square is bounded on the northern side by the open loggia of the Palazzo della Ragione (13th century) altered and restored after the fire that destroyed Giotto's frescos in 1420. In the enormous hall on the first floor are frescos attributed to Giusto de' Menabuoi. On the western side, in the adjoining square (Piazza dei Signori) is the Torre del Campanile (Falconetto, 1532) and the Palazzo del Capitano del Popolo, the residence of the Carraras, Lords of Padua until it was conquered by Venice.

Cappella degli Scrovegni (10)
piazza Eremitani 8, 35100 ☎ 049 8204550 ➠ 049 8204585

🕙 visit by arrangement: by fax: 9am–6.40pm, group tour every 20 mins ● 12,000 lire

A modest chapel, built of brick for Enrico Scrovegni in 1303–1305, houses the masterpiece of Giotto's artistic maturity: his narration of the story of Mary and Jesus which unfolds in thirty-eight paintings arranged in three rows, one above the other, along the walls of the chapel.

Prato della Valle (11)

A square of arresting scale and size (953,900 sq ft) with a number of impressive statues (seventy-eight in total) of famous people, sculpted during the years 1775–1838. The theatrical effect is enhanced by water: engineering works masterminded by Domenico Cerato diverted a branch of the River Bacchiglione through the square. ★ To the southeast stands the very noteworthy basilica of St Justinia with its abbey buildings, an important example of 16th-century architecture.

Orto Botanico (12)
via Orto Botanico 15, 35100 ☎ 049 656614

🕙 Apr.–Oct.: 9am–1pm, 3–6pm; Nov–Mar.: 9am–1pm; closed Sat., Sun. ● 5,000 lire

The world's oldest botanical gardens cover nearly 182,000 sq ft. They belong to the university, which established them in 1545 for the cultivation of medicinal plants. Among the 75,000 species is 'Goethe's palm', named after the German poet, who was inspired by his contemplation of it in 1786.

Basilica di Sant'Antonio (13)
piazza del Santo, 35100 ☎ 049 8242811

🕙 7am–7pm ● free

Built from 1232 onwards to house the bones of St Anthony, who had died in Padua the previous year. ★ Donatello sculpted the high altar and the crucifix and adorned the square with his famous equestrian statue of the illustrious condottiere, nicknamed Gattamelata.

Not forgetting

■ **Antico Brolo** corso Milano 22, 35100 ☎ 049 664555 🕙 noon–2pm, 7–10pm; closed Mon. Creative cooking ■ **Caffè Pedrocchi** via 8 Febbraio 1848 15, 35100 ☎ 049 8781231 🕙 8am–11.30pm. Historic café which has played an important role in the town's cultural life.

ministry influenced its destiny. The principal reasons today for its renown are the university – where Galileò and Kepler taught – and St Anthony.

12

12

9

13

11

Vicenza is noteworthy for Andrea Palladio's architectural gems; the historic center's most important street is named after him. In the 16th century, this small, prosperous city enjoyed a rich cultural life and acquired many exceptionally fine examples of his artistic genius. Outside the town center, beyond the Rotunda, Tiepolo's superb frescos make

Further afield

Basilica (14)
piazza dei Signori, 36100 ☎ 0444 323681

🕒 *vary depending on exhibition in progress* ● *varies*

★ In 1546 Palladio designed the loggia on three sides of the square, giving the existing group of Gothic buildings a classical aspect. North of the basilica, the Torre della Piazza (15th–16th centuries) rises to 268 ft.

Santa Corona (15)
contra' Santa Corona, 36100 ☎ 0444 323644

🕒 *8.30am–noon, 2.30–6.30pm* ● *free* **Museums of Santa Corona**
🕒 *9am–5pm; closed Mon.* ● *12,000 lire; ticket also valid for municipal museum and Teatro Olimpico*

This church's name comes from the relic that it was built to contain in 1260–70: a thorn from Christ's crown of thorns. Inside the church, there is an *Adoration of the Magi* by Veronese, and Giovanni Bellini's *Baptism of Jesus*. The adjoining monastery houses Vicenza's municipal museum's departments of natural sciences and archeology.

Palazzo Chiericati (16)
piazza Matteotti 37, 36100 ☎ 0444 321348

Municipal museum and art gallery 🕒 ● *see Santa Corona*

Designed by Palladio in 1550, the building was completed after 1660, when the sculptural decoration of the façade was added. Since 1839 it has housed Vicenza's main museum (the art collection includes a *Calvary* by Hans Memling and works by Bartolomeo Montagna).

Teatro Olimpico (17)
piazza Matteotti, 36100 ☎ 0444 222800

🕒 ● *see Santa Corona* @ *www.olimpico.vicenza.it*

Built in 1580 to Palladio's design: the thirteen stepped levels in the semi-elliptical room culminate in a Corinthian colonnade surmounted by statues added in 1751. In 1584 Vicenzo Scamozzi completed the Teatro Olimpico and also designed fixed stage sets for the Sophoclean tragedy *Oedipus Rex* which was performed to inaugurate the Olympic Theater in 1585.

La Rotonda (18)
via Rotonda 29, 36100 ☎ 0444 321793

🕒 *Mar.15-Oct.15: Tue.–Thu. 10am–noon, 3–6pm* ● *5,000 lire (exterior only), 10,000 lire*

The Villa Almerico-Capra (Palladio 1567) takes its name of La Rotonda from the great central room surmounted by a dome (Scamozzi, 1606).

Not forgetting

■ **Trattoria Tre Visi** corso Palladio 25, 36100 ☎ 0444 324868 🕒 12.30–2.30pm, 7.30pm–1am; closed Sun. evening, Mon., July. *Regional cuisine.*
■ **Pasticceria Sorarù** piazzetta Palladio 17, 36100 ☎ 0444 320915 🕒 8.30am–1pm, 3.30–8pm; closed Mon. *An old-established patisserie.*

the Villa ai Nani well worth a
detour.

16

Vicenza

14

14

15

18

17

An abundance of antique dealers
Admirers of period furniture, old master paintings and objets d'art should pay a visit to the Salizzada San Samuele, an area where many antique shops and art galleries are concentrated.

➡ Where to shop

Sales
Stores in Venice normally have sales twice a year: in January and February for the winter fashions; and in July and August for spring and summer.

Designer labels

For those with a penchant for Italian styles and fashions, the major designers have set up shop not a stone's throw from Piazza San Marco, around the Salizzada San Moisè and the Frezzeria.

49 Shops

Markets

The Sacca Fisola market is held every Friday, selling everything from clothes to vegetables. There is a daily fish market, at the Pescaria ➡ 94, and four daily fruit and vegetable markets: the Erbaria ➡ 94 at the Rialto (get there early in the morning if you want to see the *topi* (barges) unloading their cargoes), Rio Terrà San Leonardo at Cannaregio, Via Garibaldi at Castello, and Campo Santa Margherita at Dorsoduro.

INDEX BY TYPE

In the area
> **Where to stay:** ➡ 20 ➡ 34
> **Where to eat:** ➡ 40 ➡ 54 ➡ 56
> **After dark:** ➡ 64 ➡ 68
> **What to see:** ➡ 78 ➡ 82 ➡ 110

➡ Where to shop

Jesurum (1)
Mercerie del Capitello, San Marco 4857, 30124 ☎ 041 5206177

San Marco **lace** 🕐 *9am–12.30pm, 3.30–7.30pm; Sat. 9am–12.30pm* 📧 📶
piazza San Marco 60/61 @ *info@jesurum.it, www.jesurum.it*

The lace sold here merits the description of a work of art. This shop is over a hundred years old and unquestionably the best place in Venice to buy handmade lace from Burano ➡ 116, as well as household linens.

Lorenzo Rubelli (2)
campo San Gallo, San Marco 1089-1091, 30124 ☎ 041 5236110

San Marco **furnishing fabrics** 🕐 *9am–12.30pm, 3.30–7.30pm; Sat. 9am–12.30pm* 📧 @ *info@rubelli.it, www.rubelli.it*

Royalty, luxury hotels and Venetian palaces order their damask and brocades here; others go for iridescent, embossed velvets. Rubelli is particularly proud of having restored the tapestries in the Doge's Palace ➡ 80. Made in very limited quantities by hand, and costing some $150/£100 a meter (3 ft), most visitors will marvel at them rather than buy.

Rolando Segalin (3)
calle dei Fuseri, San Marco 4365, 30124 ☎ 041 5222115

Rialto, San Marco **shoes** 🕐 *9.30am–12.30pm, 3.30–7.30pm; Sat. 9am–12.30pm* 📧

Success has not spoiled Rolando Segalin: he greets all his customers with the same warmth in his amazing shop-cum-workroom, where he hand crafts reproductions of 18th-century shoes. He also takes orders for made-to-measure shoes in more contemporary styles, using all sorts of materials. Allow at least one month's waiting time and about $1,500/£1,000!

Paola e Mario Bevilacqua (4)
calle Canonica, San Marco 337/B, 30124 ☎ 041 5287581

San Marco **fabrics** 🕐 *10am–7pm* 📧

This offshoot of the textile manufacturer, Bevilacqua ➡ 144 does its parent company proud; customers can fulfill their wildest dreams for soft furnishings provided money is no object! Those on a more modest budget may let themselves be tempted by a little purse in silk damask.

Not forgetting

■ **Sigfrido Cipolato (5)** calle Casselleria, Castello 5336, 30122 ☎ 041 5228437 🕐 11am–8pm; closed Mon. 📧 *Modern Venetian jewelry.*
■ **Max Art Shop (6)** Frezzeria, San Marco 1232, 30124 ☎ 041 5287543 🕐 10am–8.30pm 📧 *Masks, puppets, collectors' dolls, costumes and objets d'art.*
■ **Paropamiso (7)** Frezzeria, San Marco 1701, 30124 ☎ 041 5227120 🕐 10.30am–8pm; closed Sun. 📧 *Period glass beads, mosaics, antique jewelry and small oriental objets d'art.* ■ **Venini (8)** piazzetta dei Leoni, San Marco 314, 30124 ☎ 041 5224045 🕐 10am–1pm, 3–7.30pm; Mon. 3–7.30pm; closed Sun. 📧 *Outlet for the Murano glassworks* ➡ 146. ■ **Mistero Atelier (9)** ruga Giuffa, Castello 4925, 30122 ☎ 041 5227797 🕐 9.30am–12.30pm 3.30–7.30pm; Nov.–Jan.: closed Sun. 📧 *Oriental silk and damask clothes, all made in Italy and designed by Alberto Curzi and Christian Cecchin.*

➡ Where to shop

Antiquus (10)
calle delle Botteghe, San Marco 2973, 30124 ☎ 041 5210106

San Samuele, Sant'Angelo **antiques and jewelry** 🕐 10am–12.30pm, 3.30–7.30pm; July 15–Aug. 15: closed Sun. ▣ ⬧ *San Marco 3131*

An elegant antiques shop, specializing in English and French furniture and glassware. Magnificent period jewelry in the adjoining shop.

Galleria Contini (11)
calle dello Spezier, San Marco 2765, 30124
☎ 041 5204942 ➡ 041 5208381

Accademia, Sant'Angelo **art gallery** 🕐 10am–1pm, 3.30–7.30pm ▣
@ galleriacontini@continiarte.com, www.continiarte.com

Contini has made its mark on the international scene, not least through its retrospectives of such artists as Gnoli, Sutherland and Igor Mitoraj.

Vittorio Trois (12)
campo San Maurizio, San Marco 2666, 30124 ☎ 041 5222905

Santa Maria del Giglio **antiques, fabrics** 🕐 10am–1pm, 4–7.30pm; Mon. 4–7.30pm; closed Sun. and Aug. ▣

Specializing in the Venetian 18th century, Vittorio Trois also has exclusivity for the much-prized Fortuny fabrics created at the beginning of the 20th century by Mario Fortuny, the Spanish painter, photographer, couturier and inventor. These fabrics are still manufactured on the island of Giudecca ➡ 92.

Piazzesi (13)
campo Santa Maria del Giglio, San Marco 2511, 30124
☎ 041 5221202 ➡ 041 5221202

Accademia, Santa Maria del Giglio **bookbinding, marbled paper** 🕐 10am–1pm, 3–7pm ▣ @ olavi@tin.it www.skyport.com/nordest/piazzesi

Venice's oldest bookbinding and paper-making firm produces sheets of marbled and stenciled paper; cards; envelopes; boxes; snakes and ladders board games, and Commedia dell'Arte figurines in papier mâché: all handmade, in limited editions.

Not forgetting

■ **Venetia Studium (14)** calle larga XXII Marzo, San Marco 2403, 30124 ☎ 041 5229281 🕐 9.30am–8pm, Sun. 10.30am–7.30pm ▣ ⬧ Mercerie, San Marco 723 ☎ 041 5229859 *A world of silks in glowing colors, paying homage to Fortuny. Their specialty is silk lampshades, hand painted and edged with Murano-glass beads.* ■ **Nalesso (15)** calle dello Spezier, San Marco 2765/D, 30124 ☎ 041 5203329 🕐 9.30am–12.30pm, 3.30–7.30pm ▣ *Specializes in recordings of classical Venetian music and doubles as a ticket office for concerts held in Venice.* ■ **Marchini (16)** ponte San Maurizio, San Marco 2796, 30124 ☎ 041 5229109 🕐 8.30am–8.30pm; closed Tue. ▣ *Traditional patisserie, including Venetian specialties like Pan dei Dogi.* ■ **Alberto Valese Ebrû (17)** campo San Stefano, San Marco 4371, 30124 ☎ 041 5238830 🕐 10am–7pm; Sat.,Sun. 11am–6pm ▣ *Still makes marbled papers in original designs by a near-eastern ('ebrù' means a cloud in Turkish) method handed down for generations and uses them to cover albums, frames and papier-mâché figures.*

17 Nalesso, one of the few shops selling recordings in Venice, also has a wide range of books on the history of music, and musical scores.

In the area
➠ **Where to stay:** ➠ 24
➠ **Where to eat:** ➠ 40 ➠ 44 ➠ 46
➠ **After dark:** ➠ 63 ➠ 66
➠ **What to see:** ➠ 82 ➠ 96

Where to shop

Valeria Bellinaso (18)
campo Sant'Aponal, San Polo 1226, 30125 ☎ 041 5223351

San Silvestro **accessories and ladies' fashions** 🕐 10am–1.30pm, 3.30–7.30pm ▭

Valeria Bellinaso designs, makes and sells extremely elegant, exceptionally fine quality ladies' accessories. Velvet purses; hats; gloves; understated, modern scarves, as well as the more traditional 'Friulian slippers' ➠ 140, all made with exquisite Italian fabrics.

Bubacco Glass Gallery (19)
**calle dell'Ogio, San Polo 1077/A, 30125
☎ 041 5225981 ➠ 041 2415091**

San Silvestro **glass sculptures** 🕐 10am–7.30pm ▭ ⑪ Studio Bubacco, fondamenta da Mula 148, Murano

As a resident of the City of the Doges, it is only fitting that Lucio Bubacco should have chosen Venice as the European showcase for his work, otherwise only on public view in large galleries in the United States. His sculptures are all executed in Murano glass, and his central theme is that of the human body in motion.

Legatoria Olbi (20)
calle della Mandola, San Marco 3653, 30124 ☎ 041 5285025

Sant'Angelo **gifts** 🕐 10am–7.30pm ▭

Paolo Olbi is a wizard with paper and leather, using very old, typically Venetian techniques: in his skilled hands these basic materials undergo a transformation into diaries, notebooks, sketch books, photo albums, writing paper, and all sorts of boxes. Some printing commissions (calling cards and invitations printed on hand-made paper) undertaken.

Atelier Laura Scocco (21)
calle della Mandola, San Marco 3654/A, 30124 ☎ 041 5231747

Sant'Angelo **mosaics** 🕐 9.30am–12.30pm, 2.10–7.30pm ▭

Visitors to this little artisan-workshop will find masks; frames; mosaics; Carnival accessories; crockery, and a very extensive range of glass tesserae guaranteed to inspire budding mosaic artists. The tiny tiles are sold by weight, in little cellophane packages; irresistible to anyone with an eye for color!

Not forgetting

■ **Targa (22)** ruga Ravano, San Polo 1050, 30125 ☎ 041 5236048 🕐 6am–8.30pm; closed Mon. and July. *Meringues come in all colors here: pistachio green, strawberry pink, vanilla, lemon and coffee, but there are also traditional cakes:* Pan dei dogi *(made with almonds and candied fruits), and* farinata, *a cake made with fine cornmeal dough, which is left to rise four times.*
■ **La Rocca-Shary (23)** calle della Cortesia, San Marco 3720/B, 30124 ☎ 041 5224245 🕐 10am–7.30pm, Mon. 3–7.30pm ▭ *Kept in a state of artful disorder, allowing customers to unearth small glass objects (rings, necklaces, perfume spray bottles) or silk scarves in a multitude of colors, and some cleverly selected garments.*

Visiting a Venetian boutique is a magical experience, not only for the merchandise on display but also because of the agreeable clutter. Such is the scarcity of space in Venice, many shops are like dolls' houses.

In the area
- **Where to stay:** ➡ 24
- **Where to eat:** ➡ 44 ➡ 46
- **After dark:** ➡ 63 ➡ 66
- **What to see:** ➡ 84 ➡ 96

➡ Where to shop

Karisma (24)
rio terrà dei Nomboli, San Polo 2752, 30125 ☎ 041 710670

San Tomà **paper and gifts** ◷ 9am–7.30pm ▣

This shop sells classic Venetian marbled paper; it also imports a cotton and cellulose paper from Madagascar, in which dried flowers and leaves are trapped between layers. Paper is not only available in sheet form (a choice of two sizes), it is also used to cover the exercise books, notebooks and albums sold here.

Tragicomica (25)
calle dei Nomboli, San Polo 2800, 30125
☎ 041 721102 ➡ 041 5240702

San Tomà **masks and costumes** ◷ 10am–7pm ▣ @ info@tragicomica.it, www.tragicomica.it ⬚ San Polo 2658

The Venetian artist, Gualtiero dall'Osto, takes pride in his prestigious client list: the Arena in Verona, the San Carlo theatre in Naples, the Regio in Turin, the Sistina in Rome and the Goldoni theatre in Venice. His masks are made to measure and come in several styles 'to suit any type of face' as he likes to remind his customers.

Livio De Marchi (26)
salizzada San Samuele, San Marco 3157/A, 30124
☎ 041 5285694 ➡ 041 5239159

San Samuele **wood sculptures** ◷ 9.30am–12.30pm, 1.30–6.30pm; closed Sat. and Sun. ▣ @ liviodemarchi@tin.it

Although his work is exhibited in art galleries all over the world, it is here, in the heart of the San Marco *sestiere* that Venetian Livio De Marchi carves his wood sculptures, reproducing full-scale models of the most familiar, everyday objects: armchairs, purses, clothes, books. Not only are his creations very accurate, they are also full of humor!

Gaggio (27)
salizzada San Samuele, San Marco 3441, 30124
☎ 041 5228574 ➡ 041 5228958

Sant'Angelo **velvets and furnishings** ◷ 9.30am–1pm, 3.30–7.30pm; closed Sun. ▣ @ www.gaggio.it

A name with a long history in the world of tapestry and furnishings, synonymous with traditional good taste and elegance. Four generations have kept to the same, time-honored oriental techniques, producing couture fabrics that are works of art (patterned velvet) for the great names of *haute couture*: Valentino, Fendi, Balestra, in Italy; Dior, Saint-Laurent, Ungaro and Givenchy in France. Gaggio uses its own stunning fabrics (fifty designs and forty colors) for cushions, sofas, ottomans, and for privileged customers' wall hangings and drapes.

Not forgetting

■ **Gallery Holly Snapp (28)** calle Crosera, San Marco 3133 ⬚ calle delle Botteghe, 30124 ☎ 041 5210030 ➡ 041 2418847 ◷ 10am–7.30pm ▣ @ snapp@unive.it *Small gallery with regular exhibitions of Venetian artists' work.*

28

The little Holly Snapp art gallery can claim credit for discovering new artistic talent in Venice.

24

25

27

26

24

In the area
- **Where to stay:** ➡ 24 ➡ 32
- **Where to eat:** ➡ 44 ➡ 52
- **After dark:** ➡ 62 ➡ 66 ➡ 68
- **What to see:** ➡ 94 ➡ 106 ➡ 108

Where to shop

La Bottega dei Mascareri (29)
ruga degli Orefici, San Polo 80, 30125 ☎ 041 5223857

▦ *Rialto* **masks** ◷ *9am–6.30pm* ▤ @ *mascareri@tin.it* 🚏 *San Polo 2720*

Sergio and Massimo Boldrin exhibit and sell their papier-mâché creations here: traditional and fantasy masks, all hand-made. Their most recent major commission was for San Francisco's Shakespeare Festival.

Brocca (30)
ruga vecchia San Giovanni, San Polo 974, 30125 ☎ 041 5225451

▦ *Rialto, San Silvestro* **men's fashion** ◷ *9.30am–7.30pm* ▤

A very wide choice of sweaters for men, by Missoni, as well as sportswear and accessories (sailing sweaters and jackets, bags, backpacks). For the casual look.

La Friulana (31)
ruga degli Orefici, San Polo 86, 30125 ☎ 041 5239833

▦ *Rialto* **typical Venetian footwear** ◷ *8.30am–7pm* ▤

'Friulane' is what Venetians call the comfortable slipper-type shoes in velvet that the gondoliers used to buy many years ago from craftsmen who came to Venice from their native Friuli province to sell their wares. Traditionally black, but now available in all sorts of colors, both here and on stalls in the Rialto market; always hand-made, with unusual soles made out of bicycle tires.

La Fucina del Ferro Battuto (32)
strada Nova, Cannaregio 4311, 30131 ☎ 041 5222436

▦ *Ca' d'Oro* **Venetian lanterns** ◷ *9.30am–1pm, 2.30–7.30pm* ▤
🚏 *Cannaregio 5045/F-5068*

The De Rossi family specializes in these typically Venetian lanterns, spheres of blown glass, enclosed in a cage of wrought iron. With many different styles, sizes and colors, hanging from the ceiling of this shop, the effect is utterly enchanting.

Lush (33)
strada Nova, Cannaregio 3822, 30121 ☎ 041 2411200

▦ *Ca' d'Oro* **soap and beauty products** ◷ *10am–8pm, Mon. 3.30–8pm* ▤

Soaps in the shape of cheeses, bath oils disguised as chocolate bars, body creams resembling pâtés, and 'fresh fruit' bath salts sold by weight: the latest fashion for natural products has been imported from England. All the stock is hand-made, using fruits, vegetables and natural extracts.

Not forgetting

■ **Pastificio Rizzo (34)** salizzada San Giovanni Crisostomo, Cannaregio 5778, 30131 ☎ 041 5222824 ➡ 041 5222824 ◷ 8.30am–1pm, 3.30–7.30pm, Wed. 8.30am–1pm; closed week of Aug. 15 ▤ *In business since 1894, making and selling homemade pastas in all shapes and colors: black (made with cuttlefish ink), green (spinach), yellow (saffron), red (tomato) and even turquoise blue (Curaçao) and violet (myrtle)!*

31

Making a Venetian lantern demands a lot of skill. Two very different basic materials and techniques are involved: glass-blowing and iron-forging.

32

29

29

30

33

In the area
- ■ Where to stay: ➡ 24 ➡ 28
- ■ Where to eat: ➡ 48
- ■ After dark: ➡ 62 ➡ 63 ➡ 68 ➡ 70
- ■ What to see: ➡ 84 ➡ 86 ➡ 88 ➡ 96

➡ Where to shop

La Ciotola (35)
crosera San Pantalon, Dorsoduro 3948, 30123

San Tomà **ceramics** 🕙 10am–12.30pm, 4–7.30pm; closed Sun.

Sybille Heller, who learned her craft in Germany, has achieved a subtle blending of Venetian tradition and contemporary creativity in her art ceramics, and in her more utilitarian china for customers' homes.

Annelie Pizzi e Ricami (36)
calle lunga San Barnaba, Dorsoduro 2748, 30123
☎ 041 5203277 ➡ 041 5203277

Ca' Rezzonico **embroidered household linen** 🕙 9.30am–12.30pm, 4–7.30pm; Sat. 9.30am–12.30pm; closed Sun.

In her romantic little boutique, Signora Annelie sells the finest quality lace and embroideries garnered from all over the world, new and second-hand: tablecloths, sheets, nightdresses, bedspreads and embroidered household linen. There are some rare, period items, such as the magnificent sheets trimmed with Burano lace.

Il Melograno (37)
campo Santa Margherita, Dorsoduro 2999, 30123 ☎ 041 5285117

Ca' Rezzonico **herbalist** 🕙 9.30am–12.30pm, 4–7.30pm

The oldest herbalist in Venice stocks a vast array of all sorts of natural products, the best Italian and foreign brands. The owner, Maria Rosaria Limongelli, is passionately interested in medicinal plants: she knows everything there is to know about their curative powers and is always trying out new formulae to soothe her clients' ills.

Giuliana Rolli (38)
salizzada San Pantalon, Santa Croce 39, 30125
☎ 041 5240789 ➡ 041 720393

San Tomà **porcelain** 🕙 9.30am–1pm, 4–8pm; closed late June–early Aug. and first week in Jan.

An attractive setting, with its exposed wood beams and 18th–19th-century furniture, for Giuliana Rolli's porcelain shop: German and French fine china, ornaments for the home, boxes, lamps, collectors' porcelain eggs, cups, plates... decorated by Giuliana herself in her studio at the back of the shop. Classical motifs (floral subjects, landscapes, animals) and more abstract decoration, inspired by Russian porcelain designs.

Mondonovo Maschere (39)
rio terrà Canal, Dorsoduro 3063, 30123
☎ 041 5287344 ➡ 041 5212633

San Basilio **masks** 🕙 10am–7pm; closed Sun.

Over six hundred papier-mâché masks, styles inspired by the Commedia dell'Arte, Greek classical theater, fables, or by the more recent source of Andy Warhol's paintings (look out for the Marilyn mask, available in several colors!). All these masks are hand-made by Guerrino Lovato who is justifiably proud of his client list, with such famous names as Stanley Kubrick, the Venetian Hotel (Las Vegas), the Kremlin… and even the Pope.

In 1993 Guerrino Lovato of Mondonovo Maschere was commissioned to make the Christmas crib that went on display in the square in front of Paris's *Hôtel de Ville*.

In the area
- **Where to stay:** ➡ 26 ➡ 30
- **Where to eat:** ➡ 46 ➡ 50
- **After dark:** ➡ 68 ➡ 70
- **What to see:** ➡ 100 ➡ 102 ➡ 106

➡ Where to shop

Luigi Bevilacqua (40)
**campiello della Comare,
Santa Croce 1320, 30125**
☎ 041 721566 ➡ 041 5242302

Riva di Biasio **furnishing fabrics** 🕐 *9.30am–12.30pm, 3–6pm; closed Sat. and Sun.* 📧 @ *bevilacqua@luigi-bevilacqua.com, www.luigi-bevilacqua.com*

Although this firm celebrated 125 years' trading in 2000, it has only been known to the public at large since 1970, the year in which the film *Goodbye Venice* was released: some of the scenes were shot in the company's workshops. The company's functioning 18th-century looms still produce the exquisite fabrics (embossed velvets, damasks and brocades) at which Venetian manufacturers excel, one of the many once-secret skills learned on long-ago journeys to the East along the silk road. Reproductions of period designs, and original creations are available, predictably at extremely high prices!

La Rifusa (41)
**campo San Geremia, Cannaregio 291
30121** ☎ 041 2750041

Ferrovia **bookshop** 🕐 *9am–8pm* 📧 🚹 *Dorsoduro 2943*

Art lovers and *aficionados* of architecture and photography will think they have gone to heaven in this bookshop: the shelves are packed with books on Venice, and on art and painting in general: all at half price! No very early works, but some books that are very hard to find elsewhere.

Rizzo (42)
rio terrà San Leonardo, Cannaregio 1355, 30121
☎ 041 718322 ➡ 041 5242745

Ferrovia, San Marcuola **patisserie** 🕐 *7.30am–8pm; closed Sun.* 📧
🚹 *San Marco 933/A, San Marco 4739, Dorsoduro 2772, Gran Viale 18-20, Lido*

For the past hundred years Rizzo has been the Venetian patisserie, even though its shops have multiplied with the passing of the years (the city now has eight Rizzo branches, in various districts)! The same passionate commitment to quality (preservatives are banned) is lavished on the local specialties produced today. In the Cannaregio shop, an entire room is devoted to candy and chocolates, and the Venetian delicacies that made this company famous: *zaletti* (little cookies made with cornmeal and raisins, sprinkled with confectioner's sugar), traditionally dipped into a glass of sweet wine; special *focacce* (round, flat cakes) made with the best butter, available from September through April; hot Carnival *fritelle* (currant fritters) and, in the fall, *favette* (little almond paste and pine nut cookies). Paradise for anyone with a sweet tooth.

Not forgetting
■ **Arte '89 (43)** rio terrà Lista di Spagna, Cannaregio 120, 30121
☎ 041 716707 🕐 9am–7.30pm; summer: 9am–10pm; closed Jan. 15–31 📧
For over forty years this shop has specialized in Murano glassware: beads and necklaces, glasses, sculpted glass ornaments in all sizes: everything is made using traditional techniques, from the millefiori items (rods of colored glass encased in transparent glass) to glassware with filigrane decoration.

Enrico Maria Salerno's movie *Goodbye Venice* (1970) starring Florinda Balkan and Tony Musante, helped to make the exclusive fabric manufacturer, Bevilacqua, known to a wider public.

40

42

43

40

In 1291 the glassmakers of Venice were ordered to quit the city for Murano ➡ 116, and take their fire risk with them. In the 15th and 16th centuries they perfected the colored glass and crystal that were to make their goblets so coveted by rich Europeans. The glassworkers of Murano are constantly refining their designs and techniques.

Where to shop

Barovier & Toso (44)
fondamenta Vetrai 28, 30141 ☎ 041 739049 ➡ 041 5274385

🔲 Colonna **art glass** 🕙 10am–12.30pm, 1–6pm; closed Mon. 🔲
@ barovier@barovier.com, www.barovier.com **Barovier & Toso Museum**
🔲 🕙 10–11am, 3–4pm and by arrangement

In 1991, the Barovier family set a record as the family with the longest continuous record of glassmaking: by then they had been contributing to the glory of Venetian glass for 700 years. Glass made by the family's most famous members are displayed in Murano's glass museum ➡ 116, among them is the wedding goblet made by Angelo Barovier. Further examples of this family's work are on show in the Barovier & Toso Museum, in the Palazzo Contarini, the company's headquarters. This houses 250 exhibits and countless archives, documenting glass production from the late 19th century to the 1970s. The exhibition gives pride of place to the works of Ercole Barovier (1889–1974) who introduced the use of color and gave a new lease of life to the art of glassmaking in Murano.

Venini (45)
fondamenta Vetrai 47-50, 30141 ☎ 041 739955 ➡ 041 739369

🔲 Colonna **art glasswork** 🕙 9am–5.30pm; closed Sat., Sun. 🔲 🛍 piazzetta dei Leoni, San Marco 314 ➡ 132 @ venini@venini.it, www.venini.it

Founded in 1921 following a meeting between a Venetian antiques dealer and a lawyer from Milan, Venini has won innumerable prizes, from the Paris exhibition of decorative arts in 1925 to the Venice Biennale in 1992. Its glassware, created by designers, such as Scarpa, Ponti, Magistretti, Sottsass and Aulenti, has contributed to the legendary reputation of Murano craftsmanship.

Carlo Moretti (46)
fondamenta Manin I/C-D, 30141 ☎ 041 736588 ➡ 041 736282

🔲 Colonna **art glasswork** 🕙 10am–5pm; closed Sun. in winter 🔲 🛍 L'Isola, campo San Moisè, San Marco 1468 ☎ 041 5231973 🕙 Apr.–Oct.: 9am–8pm; Nov.–Mar.: 9am–1pm, 3.30–7.30pm @ cmorett@tin.it

Descended from a long line of glassblowers, Carlo Moretti embarked on his own quest in 1958: how to recreate the outstanding transparency of Murano 'crystal' from a much earlier period. His success led to the acquisition of his creations by international museums as examples of innovative design and technical research.

Not forgetting

■ **Archimede Seguso (47)** fondamenta Serenella 18, 30141
☎ 041 739065 🕙 by arrangement 🔲 🛍 piazza San Marco 143
☎ 041 739065 🕙 9am–7pm. Since 1946, Seguso has been renowned for his filigrane glass and latticino work (opaque, milky white glass, and transparent glass).
■ **La Murrina (48)** pontile alla Colonna 1, 30141 ☎ 041 52744605
🕙 9.30am–noon, 2–5pm, Sat. 9.30am–1pm, 2–5pm 🔲 🛍 Riva Longa 17
☎ 041 739255 Synonymous since 1968 with lighting: Venetian-style chandeliers, also spotlights and halogen lamps in very contemporary styles.
■ **Piero Ragazzi (49)** ramo da Mula 156 🕙 8.30am–12.30pm,
2.30–5.30pm ☎ 041 736818 Specializing in murrine and colored blown glass.

48

44

45

46

47

48

48

46

46

46

Venetian place names

The wording on street signs is often in the Venetian dialect. For the sake of consistency with the addresses quoted, the standard Italian spelling has generally been adopted throughout this guide and in the map section.

➡ Finding your way

'Sestieri'

Venice is divided into 6 *sestieri* (districts): Castello, the largest; Cannaregio; Dorsoduro; San Marco; San Polo and Santa Croce. Buildings are numbered in sequence by *sestiere*, not by street (for example San Polo 1232 or San Marco 2315). It therefore helps to have as much information as possible about the exact location of the place you wish to find.

Beware of similar-sounding names

The names of many of the city's *calli* (streets) derive from the activities that formerly went on there or from their position in relation to an important building. Hence there are several 'calli del Forno' (baker's oven street) and 'drio la Chiesa' (behind the church). Therefore be sure to obtain the name of the *sestiere* and the number!

5
Maps

Street vocabulary

Calle : the Venetian for street, originally unpaved.
Campiello : small square.
Campo : square (literally 'field').
Corte : courtyard shared by a number of houses, reached by a *sottoportego* (covered passageway).
Fondamenta : quay alongside a canal.
Rio terrà : canal filled in to make a street.
Riva : quay wider than a *fondamenta*, where ships could moor in former times.
Ruga : street, similar to *calle* or *ramo* (very short).
Salizzada : major paved street.

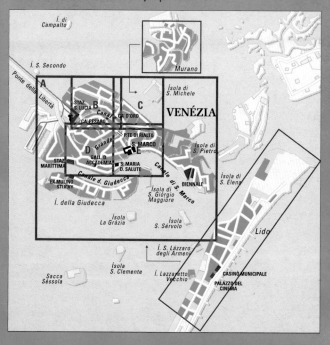

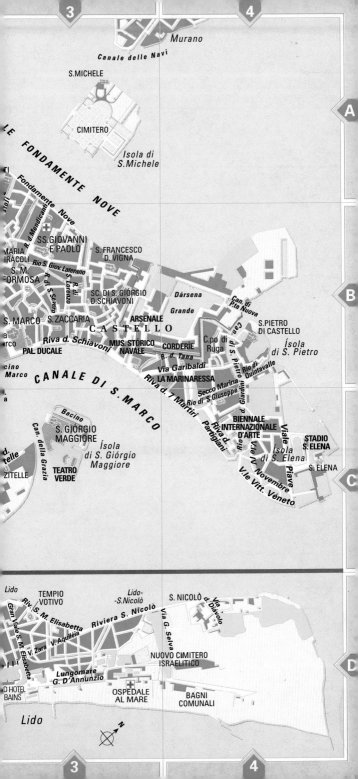

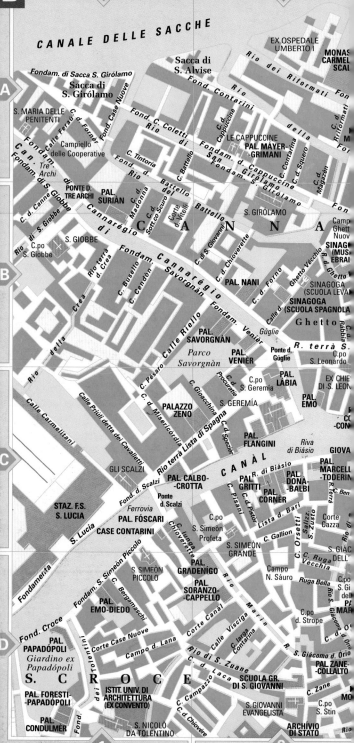

B

1 **2**

CANALE DELLE SACCHE

EX OSPEDALE
UMBERTO I

MONAS
CARMEL
SCAL

Sacca di
S. Alvise

Rio dei Riformati

Fon

Rio

A

Fondam. di Sacca S. Girólamo
Sacca di
S. Girólamo
Fond. Contarini
della
Fon

S. MARIA DELLE
PENITENTI
Fond. C. Coletti
di
Rio

Calle Ferau
C. d. Forner
Fond. Case Nuove
Fond. C. Cappuccine
LE CAPPUCCINE
PAL. MÁYER-
GRIMANI
C. d. Riformati
Fo

Campiello
delle Cooperative
C. Tintoria
Fond. d. Cappuccine
C. d. Contarina
C. d. Squero
C. d. Magazen
Fon

Fondam. di S. Giobbe
Can. Tre
Archi
C. d. Canne
Fond. d. Rio
Battello del
Fondam. di Girólamo

**PONTE D.
TRE ARCHI**
**PAL.
SURIÀN**
Cannarégio
C. d. Madonna
C. Sott.co Scuro
Corte
d'Vitelli
Battello del
S. GIRÓLAMO

C. d. Canne
di S. Giobbe
di
C A N N A
N A
Camp
Ghett
Nuov

Rio
C.po
S. Giobbe
S. GIOBBE
Rio terrà
d. Crea
C. busello
C. cendon
C. d. S. Giovanni
C. d. Chioverette
C. d. Forno
Ghetto Vecchio
R. d. Ghetto
**SINAG
(MUS
EBRAI**

B
della
Crea
Fondam.
Cannarégio
Savorgnàn
PAL. NANI
SINAGOGA
(SCUOLA LEVA

Rio
Calle Riello
Fondam.
Venier
**SINAGOGA
(SCUOLA SPAGNOLA**

della
C. Pésaro
**PAL.
SAVORGNÀN**
Gúglie
G h e t t o
C. d.
Rabbia

Parco
Savorgnàn
**PAL.
VENIER**
Ponte d.
Gúglie
R. terrà S.
C.po
S. Leonardo

Rio
Calle Carmelitani
Calle Prùli detta dei Cavalletti
C. d.
Procuratie
C.po
S. Geremia
EX CHIE
DI S. LEON

C. Gioacchina
C. d. Misericórdia
Rio terrà Lista di Spagna
C. d. Spezier
S. GEREMÍA
**PAL.
LÁBIA**
**PAL.
EMO**
CC
-CON

**PALAZZO
ZENO**

C
GLI SCALZI
PAL. FLANGINI
Riva
di Biásio
GIOVA

**STAZ. F.S.
S. LUCIA**
Fond. d. Scalzi
Ponte
d. Scalzi
**PAL. CALBO-
-CROTTA**
C A N À L
R. di Biásio
**PAL.
GRITTI**
R. di Biásio
**PAL.
DONÀ-
-BALBI**
**PAL.
MARCELL
-TODERI**

Ferrovia
PAL. FÓSCARI
C. Pisani
C. d. Pistor
**PAL.
CORNÈR**
C. Ben
R. terrà

S. LUCIA
CASE CONTARINI
C. lunga
Chioverette
C.po
S. Simeón
Profeta
Lista di Bari
C. Orsetti
Saliz.
C. Zusto
Corte
Cazza

C. Bergamaschi
**S. SIMEÓN
PICCOLO**
S. SIMEÓN
PICCOLO
**PAL.
GRADENÍGO**
S. SIMEÓN
GRANDE
C. Gallion
S. GIÁC
DELL

Fondam. S. Simeón Piccolo
Fondamenta
**PAL.
SORANZO-
CAPPELLO**
Campo
N. Sáuro
C. Ruga
Vecchia
Ruga Bella
C.po
S. Gi
dell
C.po
MAR
C. Giacomo d. Ório

D
Fond. Croce
**PAL.
EMO-DIEDO**
Rio
Marin
Corte Canàl
Calle Visciga
C. larga
Contarina

**PAL.
PAPADÓPOLI**
dei Tolentini
Corte Case Nuove
Campo d. Lana
Rio di S. Zuane
R. S. Giácomo d. Ório
**PAL. ZANE-
-COLLALTO**

Giardino ex
Papadópoli
S. Fond.
C R O C E
C. d. Laca
C. Campazzo
C. d. Chiovère
C. larga
SCUOLA GR.
DI S. GIOVANNI
C.po
d. Strope
C. Zane

**PAL. FORESTI-
-PAPADÓPOLI**
**ISTIT. UNIV. DI
ARCHITETTURA
(EX CONVENTO)**
S. GIOVANNI
EVANGELISTA
C.po
Stin
MO

**PAL.
CONDULMER**
S. NICOLÒ
DA TOLENTINO
**ARCHÍVIO
DI STATO**
Rio

1 **2**

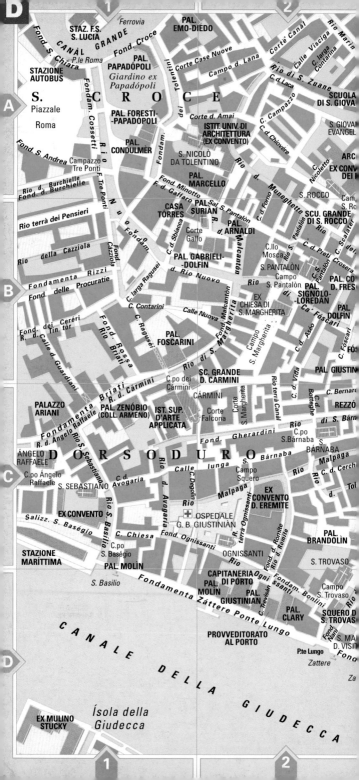

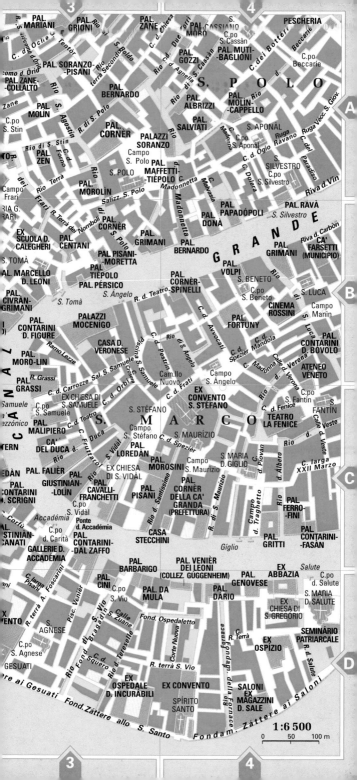

For each street, the letter in bold refers to one of the maps (**A**–**E**), and the letters and numbers mark the corresponding square in which it is found.

Street
index

Vaporetti map

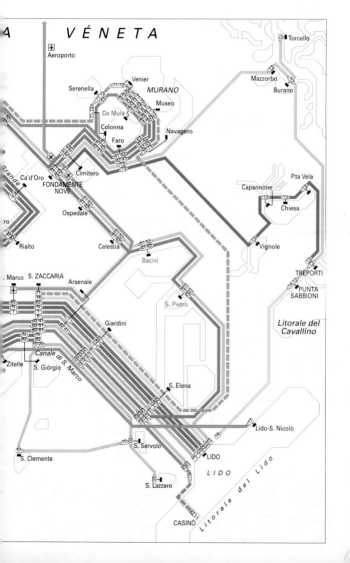

See pages 6–15 for practical information about getting there, getting around and getting by.

General
Index